DC COMICS

HARLEY QUINN™

WILD CARD

By Liz Marsham

Illustrated by Patrick Spaziante

Harley Quinn created by Paul Dini and Bruce Timm

SCHOLASTIC INC.

Copyright © 2016 DC Comics. BATMAN and all related characters and elements are trademarks of and © DC Comics. (s16)

All rights reserved. Published by Scholastic Inc., *Publishers since 1920*. SCHOLASTIC and associated logos are trademarks and/or registered trademarks of Scholastic Inc.

The publisher does not have any control over and does not assume any responsibility for author or third-party websites or their content.

This book is a work of fiction. Names, characters, places, and incidents are either the product of the author's imagination or are used fictitiously, and any resemblance to actual persons, living or dead, business establishments, events, or locales is entirely coincidental.

ISBN 978-1-338-03071-6

10 9 8 7 6 5 4 3 2 1   16 17 18 19 20

Printed in the U.S.A.   40
First printing 2016

Book design by Rick DeMonico

CONTENTS

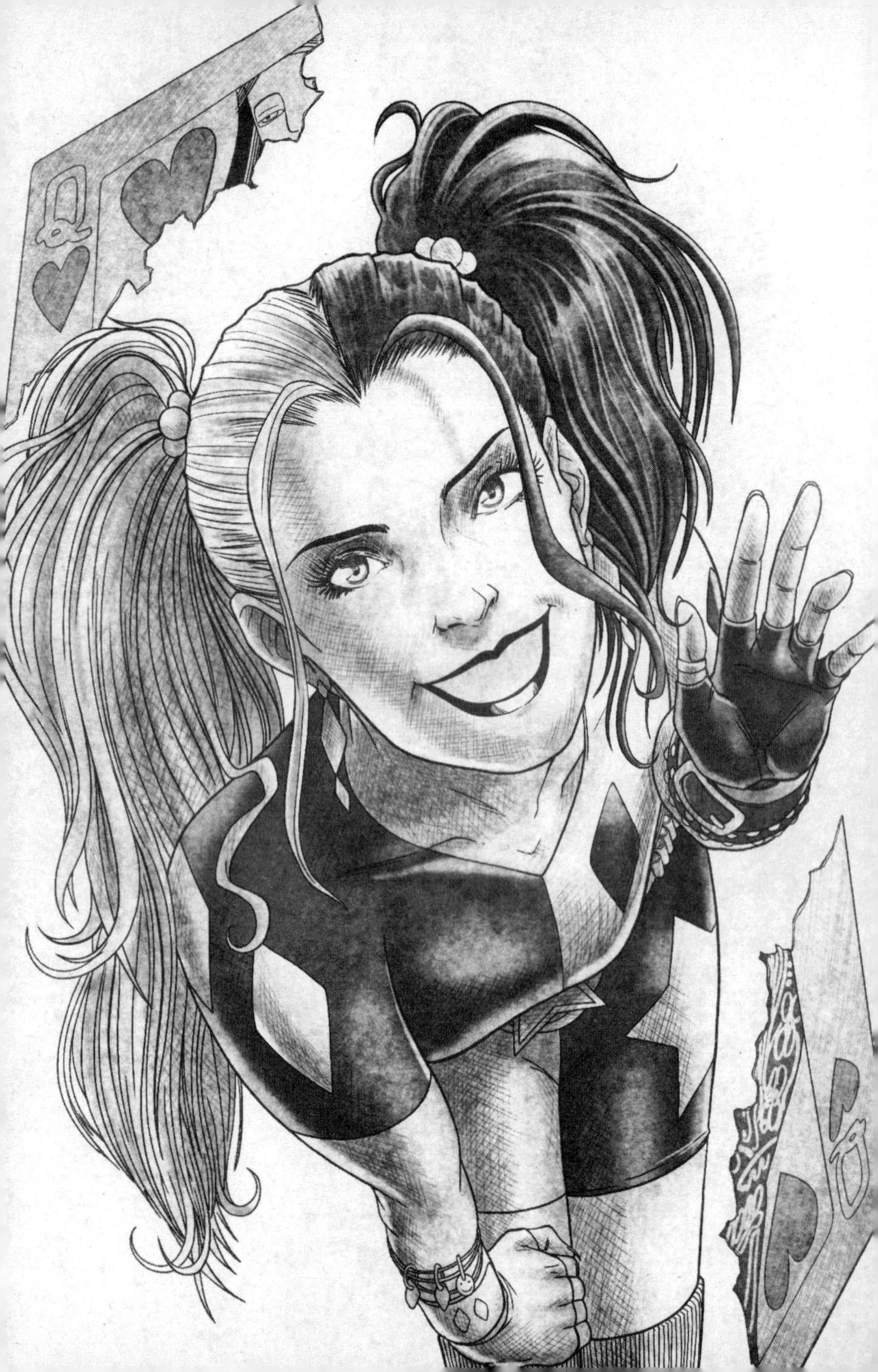

Foreword
by Harley Quinn

O h, hi! Would ya look at this? Someone decided to write a book all about me!?

Not that I'm surprised. My life is pretty interesting. And not just the part you may already know about, when I dated a really bad guy for a while. There's a lot more to me than that.

My life is all about taking lemons and making lemonade. Or, if I don't feel like lemonade, taking lemons and rubbing lemon juice all around the rim of someone's coffee cup. (Then when they drink, they get a mouthful of sour they didn't expect. Ha, their face! That one always makes me smile.)

Sorry, I got off track for a second. Look, the point is, I've been through all kinds of stuff. Some of it was great, and some of it was not so great. But I got through it, and I kept finding the fun, and I made things work out for me.

Now, let's talk about this book. I know a thing or two about writing books—after all, I've written one myself! (Betcha didn't know that, huh? See, there's lots to me! Layers and layers! Like an onion. Except less stinky. Wait, what was I saying? Oh yeah, this book.) So as soon as I found out this book was happening, I insisted on helping out. The book people were a little hesitant to let me help at first, but I talked them into it. I'm good at talking people into things!

Turns out they did a pretty good job telling my story. It needed a little extra something here and there, but don't worry, I fixed it for you—I added my notes as I went along. And as an extra-DOUBLE-special bonus, I loaned them some things from my scrapbook! They used most of them . . . but for some reason they didn't want to put in my special stink bomb recipe. Oh well.

Anyway, there's some real positive stuff in here about figuring out who you are and being that person no matter what. But there's also plenty of fun and pictures, and at one point there's a bomb. (A *deactivated* bomb, okay? Calm down, parents. Sheesh.) I think you're gonna like it. Let's get to it!

Friends, Foes, and Family

The Quinzels

Harley's mother, father, and three younger brothers. They live in Canarsie, Brooklyn. While her dad commits petty crimes for money, her mom stays at home and looks after the kids.

Dr. Joan Leland

Head of the psychiatric program at Arkham Asylum. She was Harley's first boss and later became her first therapist.

The Joker

A dangerous criminal obsessed with creating chaos. He was Harley's patient at Arkham until she set him free and they began dating.

MR. J. AKA
A BIG MISTAKE

MY BABIES!!!!

Bud & Lou

Harley's beloved pet hyenas. They are wild animals, vicious and mean to everyone except Harley.

B-MAN!

Batman

A Super Hero who protects Gotham City from criminals. Batman is the Joker's greatest enemy.

Robin

Batman's young sidekick. Robin often helps Batman catch criminals like the Joker.

RED

Poison Ivy

A super-villain with the power to control plants, and Harley's best friend. Her real name is Pamela Isley.

Kitty!

Catwoman

A super-villain and jewel thief who is friends with Harley and Poison Ivy. Her real name is Selina Kyle.

Amanda Waller

A high-ranking government official. Director of the Suicide Squad, a team of criminals who work for the government in exchange for time off their prison sentences.

Captain Boomerang

Member of the Suicide Squad. This old-fashioned super-villain uses an arsenal of trick boomerangs to take down his enemies.

Deadshot

Member of the Suicide Squad. His real name is Floyd Lawton. He is more accurate with a gun than anyone else in the world.

King Shark

Member of the Suicide Squad. No one knows the true origins of the mutated man-shark. His unique body and abilities allow him to breathe underwater and regenerate lost limbs.

Chronology

Nick and Sharon Quinzel have their first child, a daughter, and name her Harleen.

Harleen grows up in Canarsie, Brooklyn, with her parents and her three younger brothers.

The Joker escapes Arkham, but is soon caught and imprisoned again. Harleen decides to free him for good.

Harleen creates a new look and identity for herself and becomes Harley Quinn.

Harley breaks the Joker out of Arkham, and the two begin dating.

Harley is released from Arkham and has difficulty making a new, "normal" life for herself.

Harley teams up with Poison Ivy and Catwoman, but she eventually makes a mistake and gets arrested.

Instead of going to prison or back to Arkham, Harley agrees to join the Suicide Squad, a team of criminals working for the government.

Harleen excels at her schoolwork, attends college and then medical school, and becomes a psychiatrist.

 Harleen gets a job at Arkham Asylum treating criminals. She especially enjoys working with an inmate known as Poison Ivy.

 Harleen becomes unhealthily obsessed with the Joker, one of her other patients.

 Harley tries to prove herself to the Joker by going on a crime spree without him.

The Joker is jealous of Harley's success and makes sure she is caught and sent to Arkham, while he remains free.

As a patient in Arkham, Harley realizes the truth about the Joker, and later even helps Batman and Robin catch him.

 Once Harley is released from working for the Squad, she is finally able to create a successful life for herself on Coney Island.

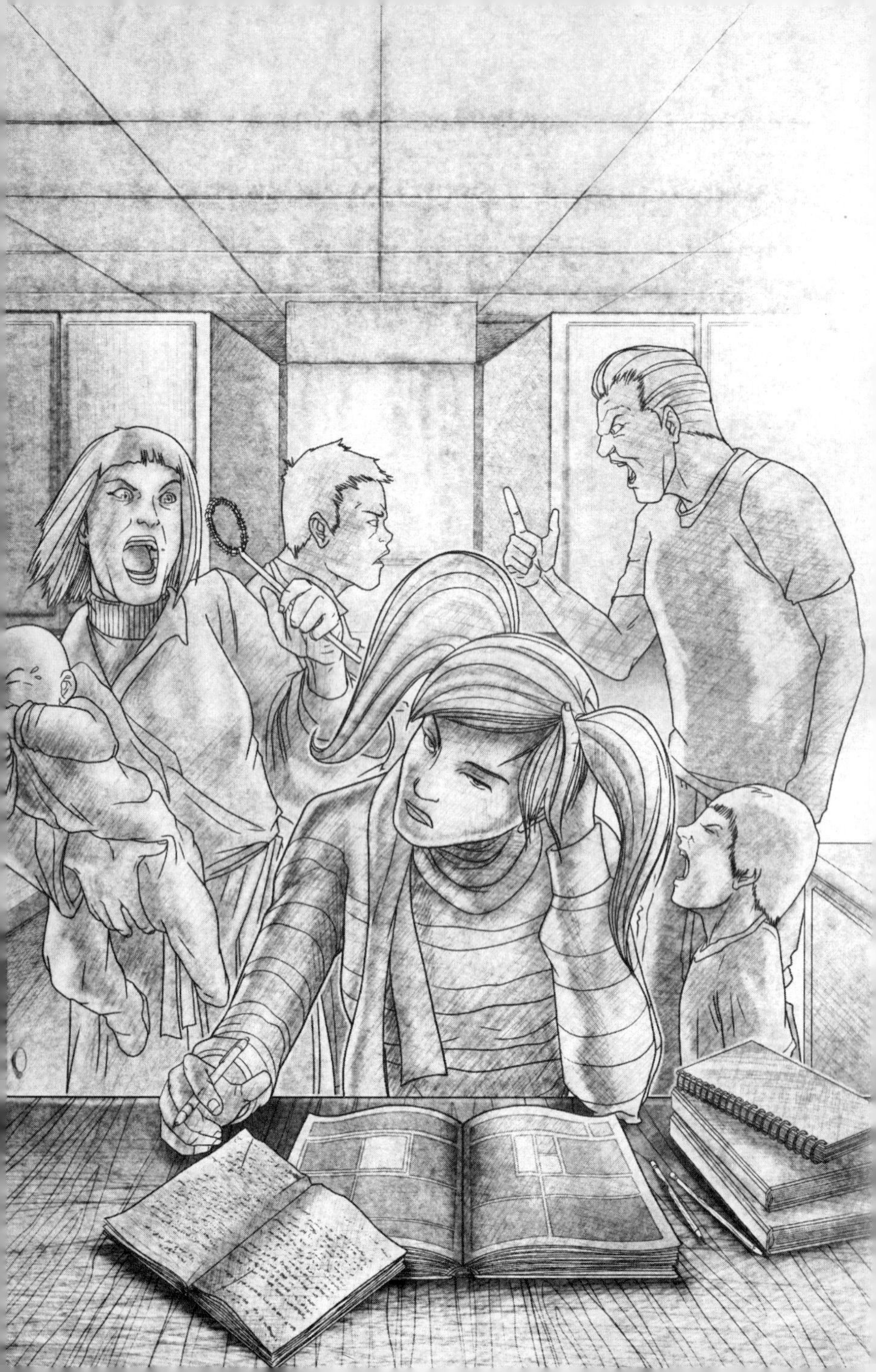

CHAPTER ONE

FAMILY HISTORY

Harleen Quinzel always stood out.

In her family, she stood out as the only girl. Their apartment in Canarsie, Brooklyn, was small, and it felt even smaller with her three noisy brothers around. Her con artist father was usually away, either tricking someone out of their money or sitting in jail. So her mother often yelled at her to help out around the house and keep her brothers in line. And since Harleen was also the only person in the family interested in getting an education, it was hard to find time to study.

She managed, though. In high school, she stood out as one of the top students in her class, and she was also the star of the gymnastics team. Harleen loved the feeling of learning something fascinating in class or mastering a tricky, new acrobatic routine—like her life was under control.

Her smarts, her natural athleticism, and her hard work paid off. When high school was over, she could take her pick of colleges. And there were plenty of scholarships available for someone with her record, so she didn't have to worry about her parents paying for her to go. She could even choose between an academic scholarship and an athletic scholarship! Harleen knew that she wanted to understand the way people's minds work, so she accepted Gotham State University's academic scholarship and enrolled in their excellent psychology department.

As she worked her way through college, Harleen soon realized why she had chosen that particular

HA, would you look at that! I forgot all about how I love that feeling! SPOILER ALERT That's Not gonna Last.

field of study. She wanted to understand people in general . . . but she especially wanted to understand people like her father. All her life, Nick Quinzel had been in and out of jail for tricking people into giving him money. Harley worried that he would even try to convince her to give him her scholarship money. What, she wondered, made someone act that way? What made someone stop caring about the law and the people around them? Could people like that be fixed?

Could she be the one to fix them?

Now Harleen had a new goal: to become a psychiatrist. She was accepted into Gotham State University's School of Medicine and focused on understanding and treating criminals and other extreme personalities. After excelling in all of her courses, she graduated medical school near the top of her class. She could officially call herself Dr. Quinzel.

The next step in her career was a residency

NEW YORK CITY POLICE DEPARTMENT

New York, NY

INCIDENT REPORT #: 977012543651

Date/Time Reported: January 21

Incident Type/Offense:

Reporting Officer:

KAUFMANN, EDWARD

Offender(s)

Name

QUINZE

Victim(s)   Name

(MULTIPLE VICTIM CO   LIST BELOW)

NYS DOCS

072A886
QUINZEL, NICHOLAS

NARRATIVE

Mr. Quinzel was brought in for questioning today after several women submitted po

reports naming him in a string of thefts. All victims were convinced to give Mr. Quin

money after Mr. Quinzel presented them a variety of false claims, excuses, and

misrepresentations.

ONE OF NICK QUINZEL'S MANY ARREST REPORTS.

Arkham Asylum

Looming near the border of Gotham City, the sprawling Arkham Asylum houses and treats some of the country's most notorious criminals. The facility is officially called the Elizabeth Arkham Asylum for the Criminally Insane, after the mother of the founder, Amadeus Arkham. Disturbing events have always haunted the asylum. For instance, both the founder and the architect became dangerously unstable during its construction, and they were eventually confined as inmates in their own building.

at a psychiatric hospital, where she would learn from more experienced doctors while beginning to treat patients of her own. Several top hospitals sent requests for the new doctor to interview with them. She was most interested in a job opening at the famous Arkham Asylum. For years, she had been reading about the criminals sent for treatment at Arkham, especially the ones caught by Batman. Those had extreme personalities, which would be a great challenge to examine and treat. Harleen set up an interview with Dr. Leland, the head of Arkham's psychiatry program.

The interview went better than Harleen could have hoped. She had exactly the kind of fresh new ideas that Dr. Leland was looking for in her treatment program. Before ten minutes had gone by, she knew that the job was hers if she wanted it.

And she did want it! As part of the interview, Dr. Leland gave her a tour of the secure wings of the asylum. Arkham's inmates did not disappoint: Each

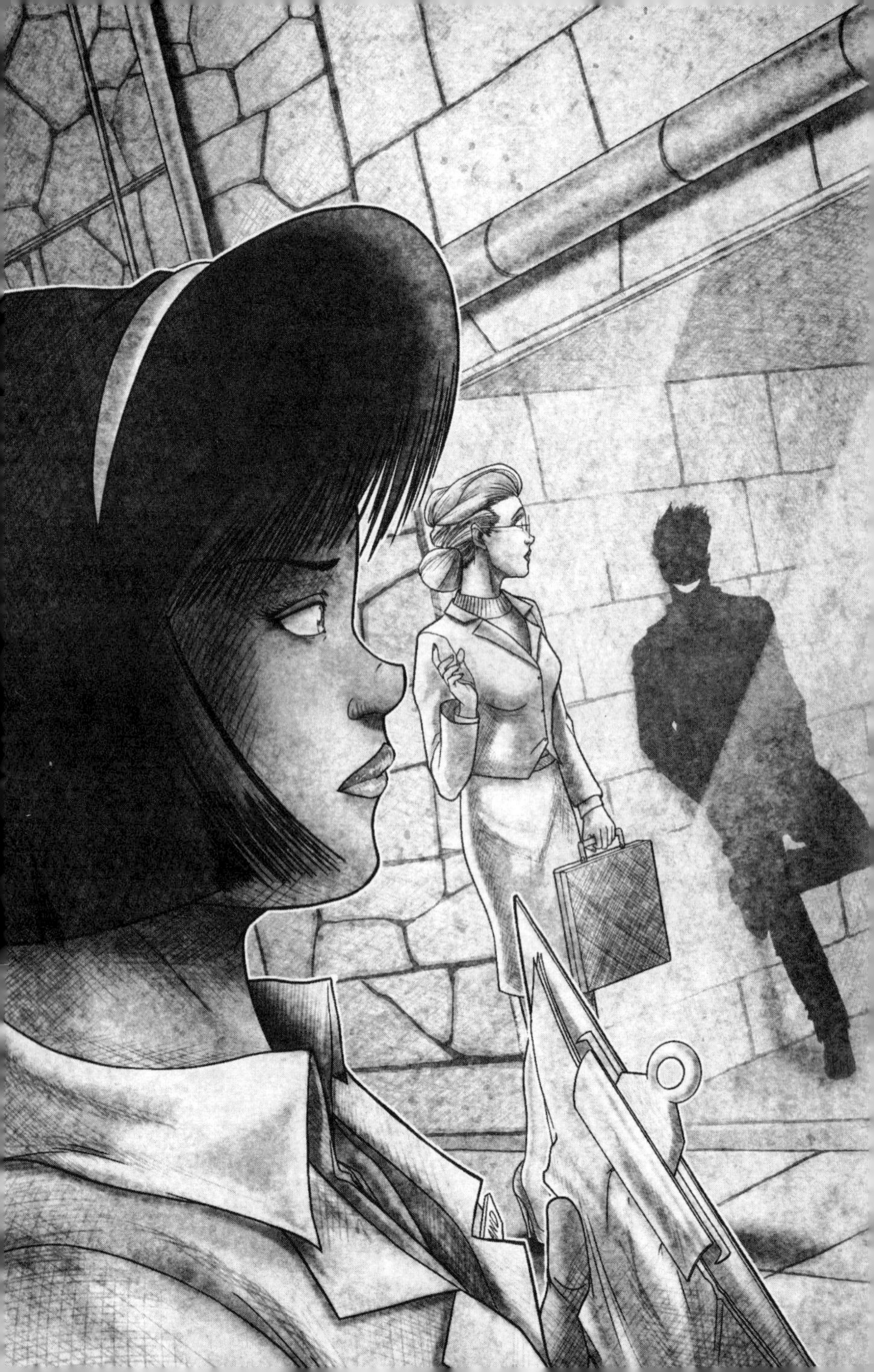

one's problems would be more of a triumph to solve than the next. There were so many patients she could help, and so many of them would make excellent material for the books she planned to write.

It seemed like Dr. Harleen Quinzel and Arkham Asylum were a perfect match. She had finally found a place where she fit right in. *See what they DID there?! That's called "Foreshadowing," kids!*

DR. QUINZEL'S STAFF BADGE FROM ARKHAM ASYLUM (LATER DEFACED).

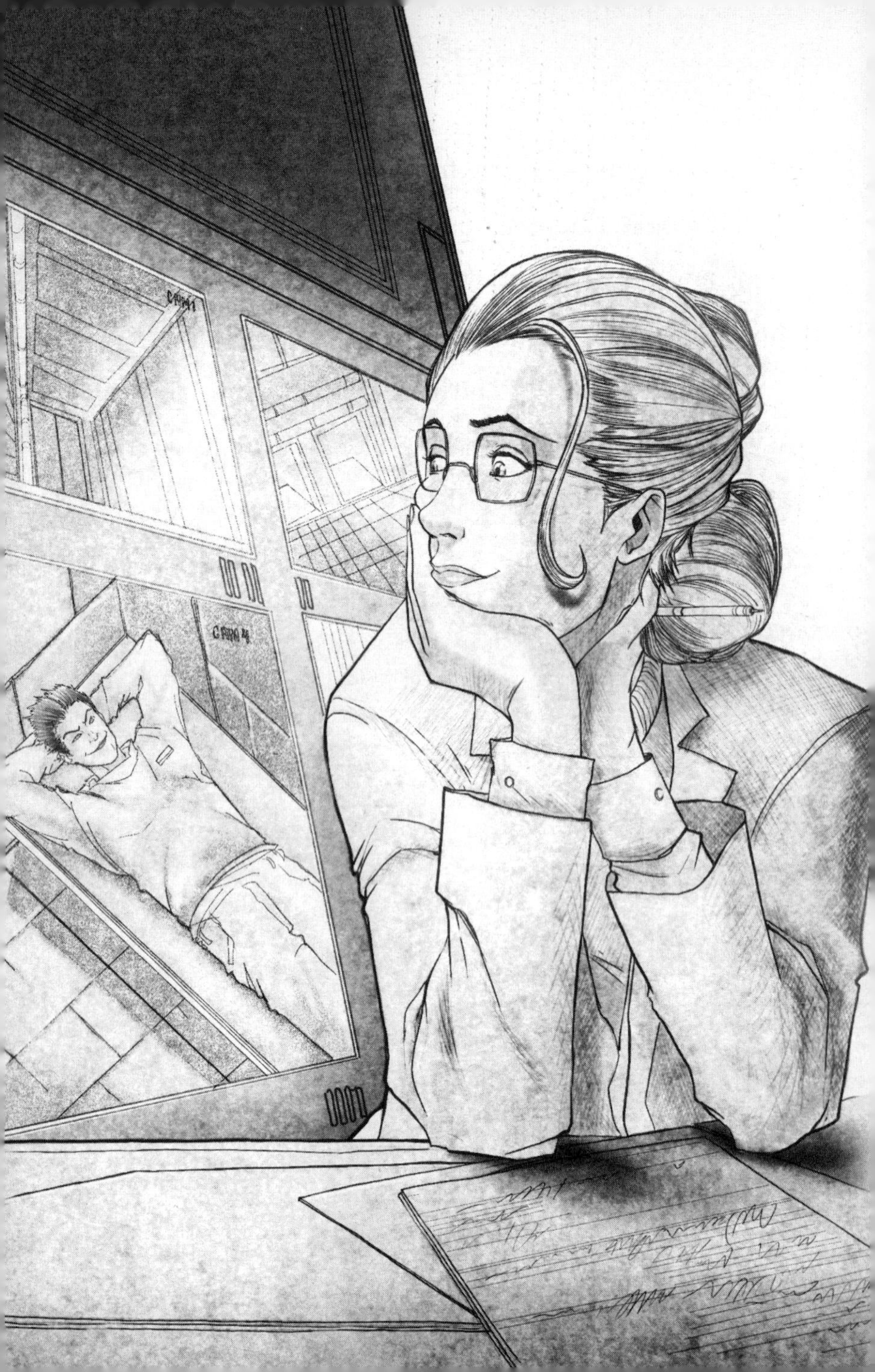

CHAPTER TWO

COUNTER-TRANSFERENCE

A year later, Harleen wasn't making the kind of progress she had hoped for. She had definitely succeeded in some things, but other parts of her work were very frustrating.

One of her greatest successes was with an inmate named Pamela Isley, more commonly known as the criminal Poison Ivy. In addition to controlling plants with her mind, Ivy could release plant scents and poisons from her skin, which she used to hypnotize or hurt people. She was used to being distrusted and very unused to being touched. So she was shocked on her first day of therapy with her new psychiatrist, when Harleen walked right up to her and offered her hand to shake.

Ivy just stared. "You know that I could concentrate enough toxins in my hand to kill you, don't you, Dr. Quinzel?"

Harleen smiled and left her hand out. "I believe that friendships should be built on a strong foundation of trust," she replied.

The two shook hands, and soon Ivy began to show rapid improvement in therapy. As a reward for Ivy's progress and new good behavior, Harleen recommended that she be allowed to start receiving mail. Harleen also had Ivy moved to a cell with a window, so the most plantlike part of Ivy could enjoy the sunlight. Ivy appreciated what Harleen was doing for her, and she began acting like a model patient.

At the same time, she found herself more and more fascinated by one of her other patients, known only as "the Joker." The Joker was a career criminal who seemed obsessed with three things: using clown- and circus-related items in his crimes, fighting Batman, and treating life like one big joke.

All the Joker's previous psychiatrists had given up on him. As Harleen read through his file, she saw notes from those other therapists, like "patient is a lost cause" and "he is incapable of and uninterested in reform." One that stood out the most to her read, "this man is a hopeless mess of symptoms with no cause and no cure."

Her own therapy sessions with the Joker showed little promise. He answered her with nonsense or outright lies, often giving entirely different answers to the same questions. She just didn't feel like she was getting through to him.

But then the Joker started sending Harleen presents. Flowers, cards, and other tokens of affection began appearing in her office, with handwritten notes that could only be from him. Was he getting out of his cell? Or had he convinced one or more of the guards to help him? Either way, she knew the official, correct thing to do: She should report him.

Knowing Mr. J?
Probably Both? HA HA!

Harleen had no intention of doing the official thing. After all, what had that gotten all those other therapists? Instead, she took the presents as a sign that the Joker was finally ready to open up to someone. Maybe this was the perfect opportunity for a new therapy technique she had been wanting to try.

He could be the sweetest thing when he wanted to be. Made it real easy to fall FOR HIM. OOPS, SPOILER!

She went to Dr. Leland and presented her idea: In order to get some of the more stubborn patients to open up to her, she should disguise herself as a fellow inmate. Dr. Leland rejected the plan immediately. It was far too dangerous. But Harleen didn't give up, bringing up her success with Ivy and other patients and pleading for Dr. Leland to trust

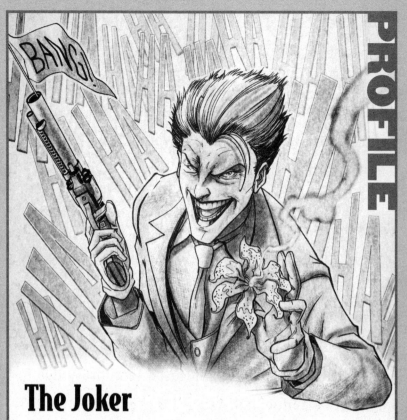

The Joker

No one knows for sure who the Joker used to be—maybe not even the Joker himself. The story goes that he was a petty criminal who fell into a vat of toxic waste while being chased through a chemical plant by Batman. Disfigured by the acidic sludge, he emerged from the vat with green hair, white skin, and an unnaturally wide smile. These changes unbalanced him mentally, and he adopted a new name and persona: the Joker, the Clown Prince of Crime. He also had a new mission: to throw Gotham City into chaos, making life as miserable as possible for his nemesis, the Batman, and showing the rest of the world what a joke life really was.

her. Eventually, Dr. Leland granted permission, but only if Harleen signed a huge stack of papers saying that everything she did was at her own risk. If anything bad happened, it wouldn't be Arkham's fault. Harleen signed gladly.

Then it was time to choose her disguise. She may have told Dr. Leland that she wanted to gain the trust of many inmates, but she really only had one patient in mind: the Joker. So she chose a look that she thought he would respond to. She took off her glasses and powdered her skin white. Next she put her hair in pigtails and used temporary dye to color it half-blue, half-red. All that plus an inmate's jumpsuit, and she looked very different from the well-dressed, conservative Dr. Quinzel.

Her plan seemed to work like a charm. From the first time they met in the prison yard, the Joker was incredibly friendly. They talked whenever the Joker was allowed out of his cell to visit the yard or the cafeteria. Soon, Harleen found herself opening up

Because of course no one recognizes you when you take your glasses off ... Right?

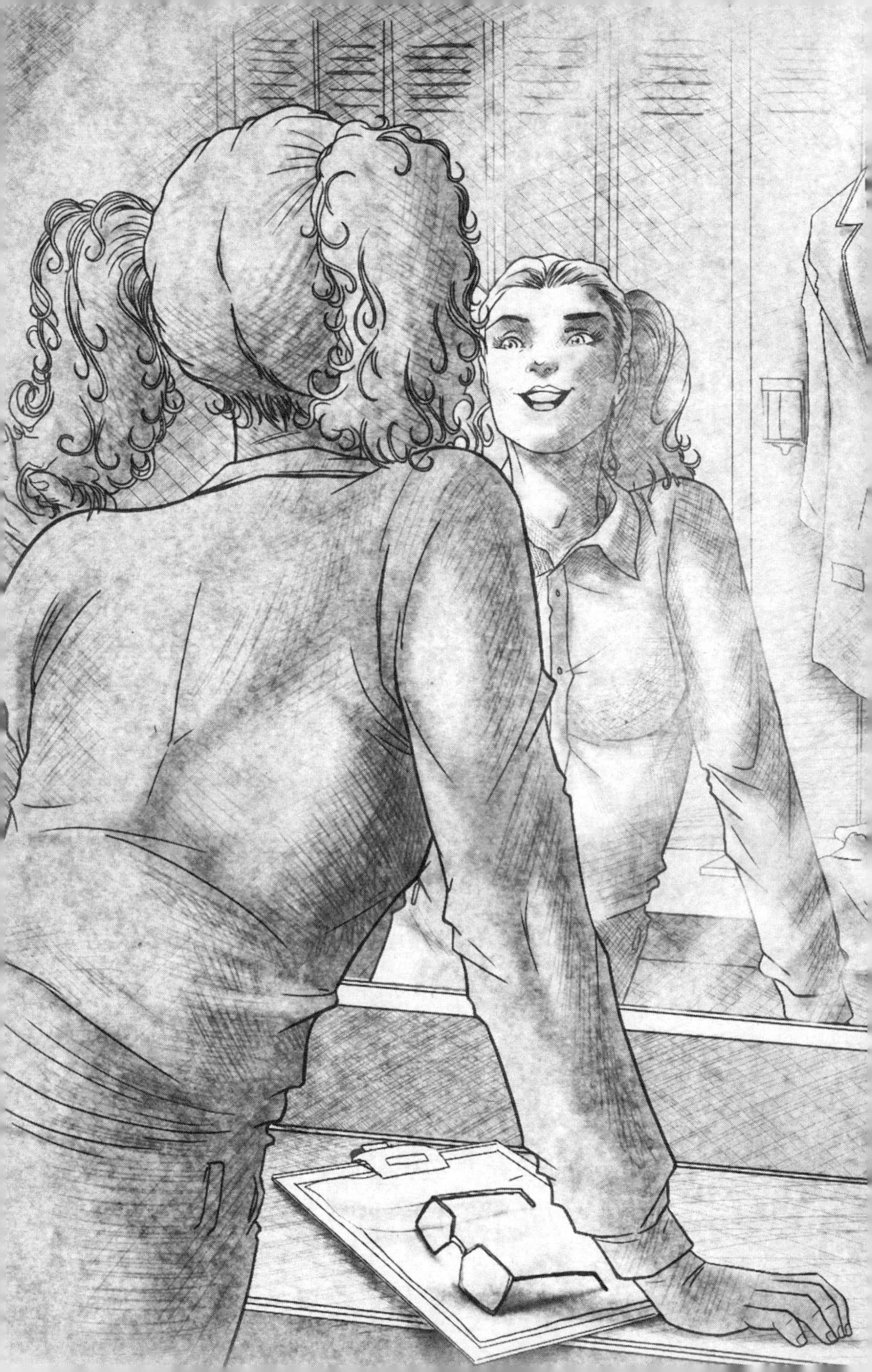

to the Joker as much, or maybe more, than he was opening up to her. He was so easy to talk to, he was such a good listener, and he made her laugh!

Harleen was now sure that the Joker had just been misunderstood. *When you really listen to him,* she thought, *he has some good points. What makes someone like Batman more qualified to decide what's "right" and "wrong" than someone like the Joker? Maybe right and wrong are more flexible than I always thought. Maybe, when you get right down to it, the whole thing is just a joke.*

MEDICAL RECORD PROGRESS NOTES

5/24 Another great conversation. Patient has remarkable insight into my family situation, plus he taught me two hilarious knock-knock jokes!

5/26 I know why other therapists failed: They tried to get him to agree to their "normal" point of view. Has anyone ever tried to understand his point of view? Turns out it's preeeeeeetty interesting.

5/30 I was very anxious to check on the patient today after the long weekend. I shouldn't have worried — he's fine!

6/2 He saved me some of his pudding at lunch. What a sweet gesture.

EXCERPT FROM DR. QUINZEL'S LATER FILES ON THE JOKER.

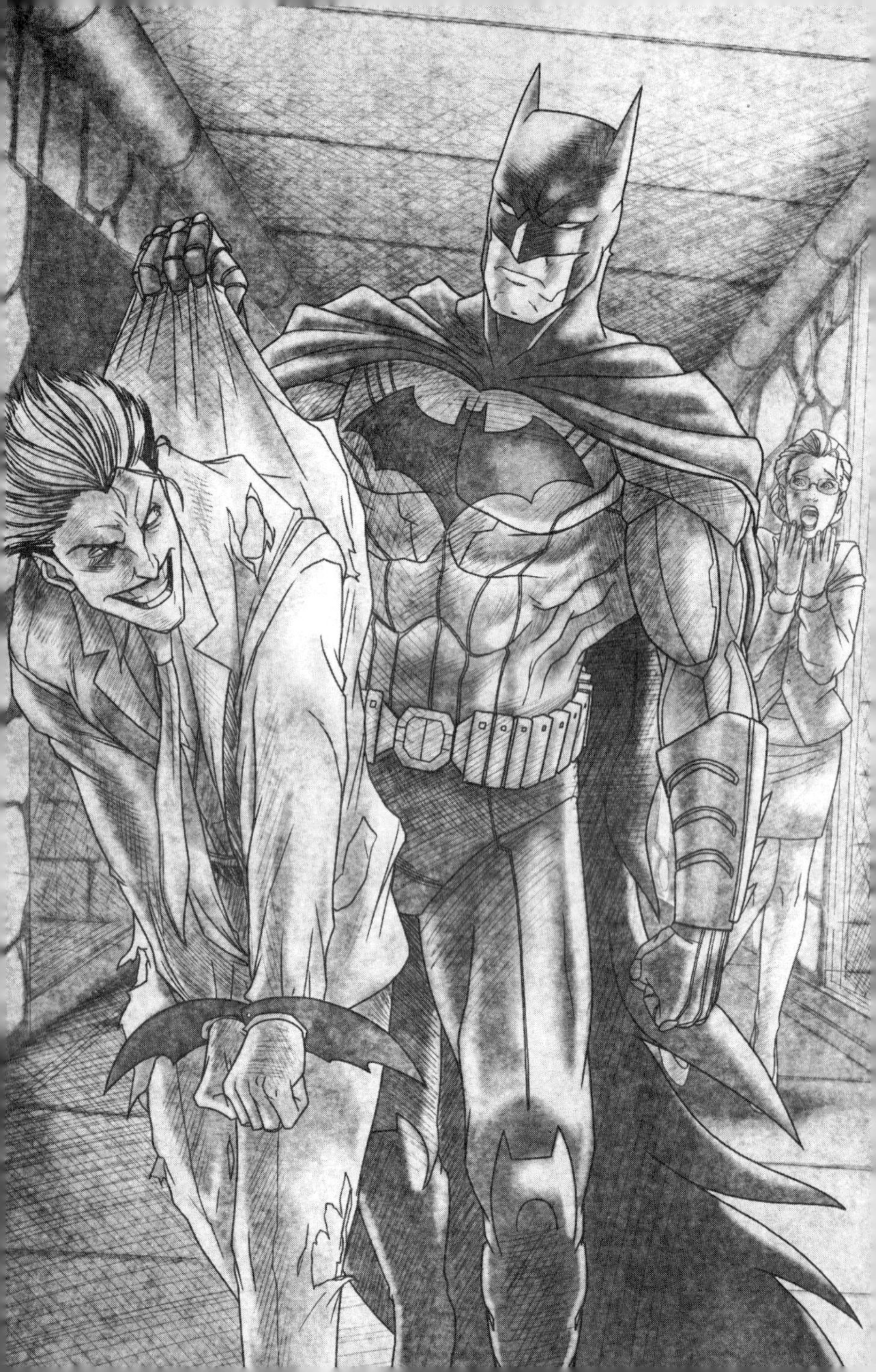

CHAPTER THREE

CODEPENDENCY

One morning, Harleen arrived at work to a terrible shock. There was the Joker, her sweet, misunderstood Joker, being dragged through the security doors at Arkham by Batman, with his face bruised up! Everyone around her was talking about how the Joker had escaped around dawn and had been captured by Batman right away. Some of the guards were even laughing about it.

Harleen couldn't believe it. She canceled all her appointments for the day and spent the whole time

JOKER'S "BANK HOLIDAY" C

Clown Prince of Crime Escapes Arkham Asylum,

search or lockdown proc
Police are investigating
the time and the alarm
Arkham security chi
that he will undertak
avoid this type of m

According to
police investigate
facility, the Jok
weapons and ec
tunnel that runs
Police were a
remains of th
traps left in
drew near,
scene and
tunnel its
mainten

The
loaded
way
causi
to w
Na
th
w

GOTHAM CITY—The super-villain known only as "the Joker" escaped from his court-mandated confinement at Arkham Asylum early this morning. In an attempted bank heist that police authorities called "haphazard at best," the Joker immediately celebrated his freedom by blowing the front doors off of the Monolith Square branch of Gotham National Bank. He was quickly apprehended by Batman and returned to Arkham.

Speculation is running rampant as to how the Joker managed to escape the locked ward at Arkham in the first place, but at the time of this reporting there is no official word. While an alarm did go off in his ward at approximately 5:30 a.m., which seems to correlate with the time of his escape, was written off as faulty wiring, and no

T SHORT BY BATMAN

ught Robbing Bank Three Hours Later

were implemented.
ne guards on duty at
n itself. Additionally,
on Cash has indicated
al procedural review to
n the future.
eline pieced together by
ce clear of the Arkham
de his way to a hidden
nt cache near the old steam
el to the New Trigate Bridge.
ollow the Joker's trail to the
e. Unfortunately, several booby
rea exploded as the task force
grating any evidence left at the
g minor structural damage to the
e area has been evacuated until a
ew can attend to any repairs.
then hijacked a garbage truck,
uipment inside, and sped the wrong
ity streets toward Monolith Square,
eral minor traffic collisions. According
s at the scene, he arrived at the Gotham
Bank branch shortly after 8 a.m., before
opened for the day. He ignored shouted
s from the security guards as he raced
steps, deposited a four-foot-high wrapped
t just outside the locked main doors, and then
for cover behind the garbage truck. Security
caught unprepared for such a brazen assault
had no choice but to take cover themselves as

the "present" exploded, leaving a jagged hole in
the main doors.

The next step of the Joker's plan remains
unclear, as at this point Batman arrived in the
Batmobile. The two engaged in a brief hand-to-
hand altercation, which the Batman quickly won.
As authorities and reporters began arriving on the
scene, Batman subdued the Joker, tied his hands,
and loaded him into the Batmobile, explaining to
the police that he would take personal responsibility
for returning the criminal to Arkham.

A few reporters had time to pose questions
to Batman and the Joker as the Batmobile doors
were closing. Batman waved off all inquiries, but
the Joker was more forthcoming. In response to the
questions, "What were you going to do next?" and
"How were you going to get into the bank past the
guards?" the Joker gave a cheery "Who knows?"

Another reporter asked, "Batman, do you
ever get tired of capturing the Joker over and over
again?" As the Batmobile door slid shut, the Joker
called back, "Are you kidding? This is Batman's
favorite game!"

An official statement from Arkham Asylum,
released at 9:30 a.m., indicates that Batman turned
the Joker over to the asylum's custody with no
further incident, and that the Joker is once again
confined to the institution. It is this reporter's
fondest hope that this time he stays there for the
full term of his sentence.

NEWSPAPER CLIPPING
DETAILING THE JOKER'S
ESCAPE AND CAPTURE
BY BATMAN.

Batman

Batman is Gotham City's protector. With his wide array of special gadgets, weapons, and vehicles, he helps the police keep the streets safe from crime. Though he doesn't have powers like Superman or Wonder Woman, he is still a Super Hero. He is a genius, and he has trained himself to be a martial arts expert, a master of technology, and an excellent detective. Even the most dangerous super-villains fear the Batman!

in her office, using the security cameras to watch the injured Joker in his cell. She thought and thought, and the more she thought, the angrier she became. Surely it was unfair for someone like Batman, someone who wasn't even officially part of the police, to beat people up and be praised for it. Harleen was convinced that the Joker couldn't possibly have done anything to deserve that treatment.

Well, that was the last straw. If Batman was allowed to take justice into his own hands, then so was Dr. Harleen Quinzel!

But when she thought about it, "Dr. Harleen Quinzel" didn't seem like the right person to be anymore. If she wanted to help the Joker, if she wanted to be in on his joke, she'd have to act the part.

First, she needed a new look. Her "inmate" outfit was a good start, but it didn't go nearly far enough. Then, she needed a new name, something that would show off her more carefree perspective. Last, she needed a foolproof plan that would kick her new life off with a bang. She stayed in her office until long after dark, plotting.

When she finally left the asylum, she drove straight to the nearest costume and novelty store. It was closed by that time, but why let that stop her? Harleen broke in through a window and ransacked the store for supplies. In her car, she stuck some things together and tore other things apart until

she had exactly what she needed. Then she raced straight back to Arkham.

Putting all those years of gymnastics training and her new novelty props to use, Harleen got past every guard in her way. Some guards she snuck

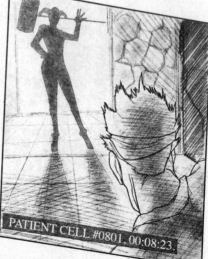

Look at me! I was a natural at this FROM the Start!

around, and some she distracted with stink bombs. When she couldn't avoid conflict, she knocked the guards over the head with a rubber chicken stuffed with sand.

Finally, she reached the Joker's cell. Inside, she saw him sleeping fitfully, his head covered in bandages.

"Get back, Mr. J!" she called to him.

The Joker woke up slowly. "Whuh? Who's there?"

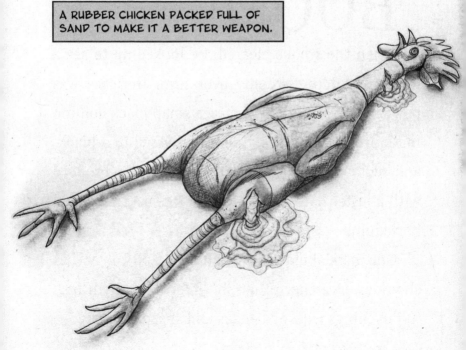

A RUBBER CHICKEN PACKED FULL OF SAND TO MAKE IT A BETTER WEAPON.

All he could see outside his cell was a dark shape.

"You'll see! But you better cover that precious head of yours first!"

The Joker took the hint and crawled under his bed for protection. Peeking out from underneath, he saw a hand stick something to the reinforced glass door of his cell. He barely had time to pull his head back under the bed before

BOOM!

When the smoke cleared, he looked up to see a woman standing proudly over him. Her face was powdered white, and she wore a small black domino mask around her eyes. She was dressed in a black-and-red outfit decorated with diamonds and topped with a jester hat, making her look like a traditional harlequin.

One hand held a huge mallet slung over her shoulder. Over her other shoulder was a gym bag, full of things with odd edges and sharp corners.

LOOK That One Up in The GLOSSARY!

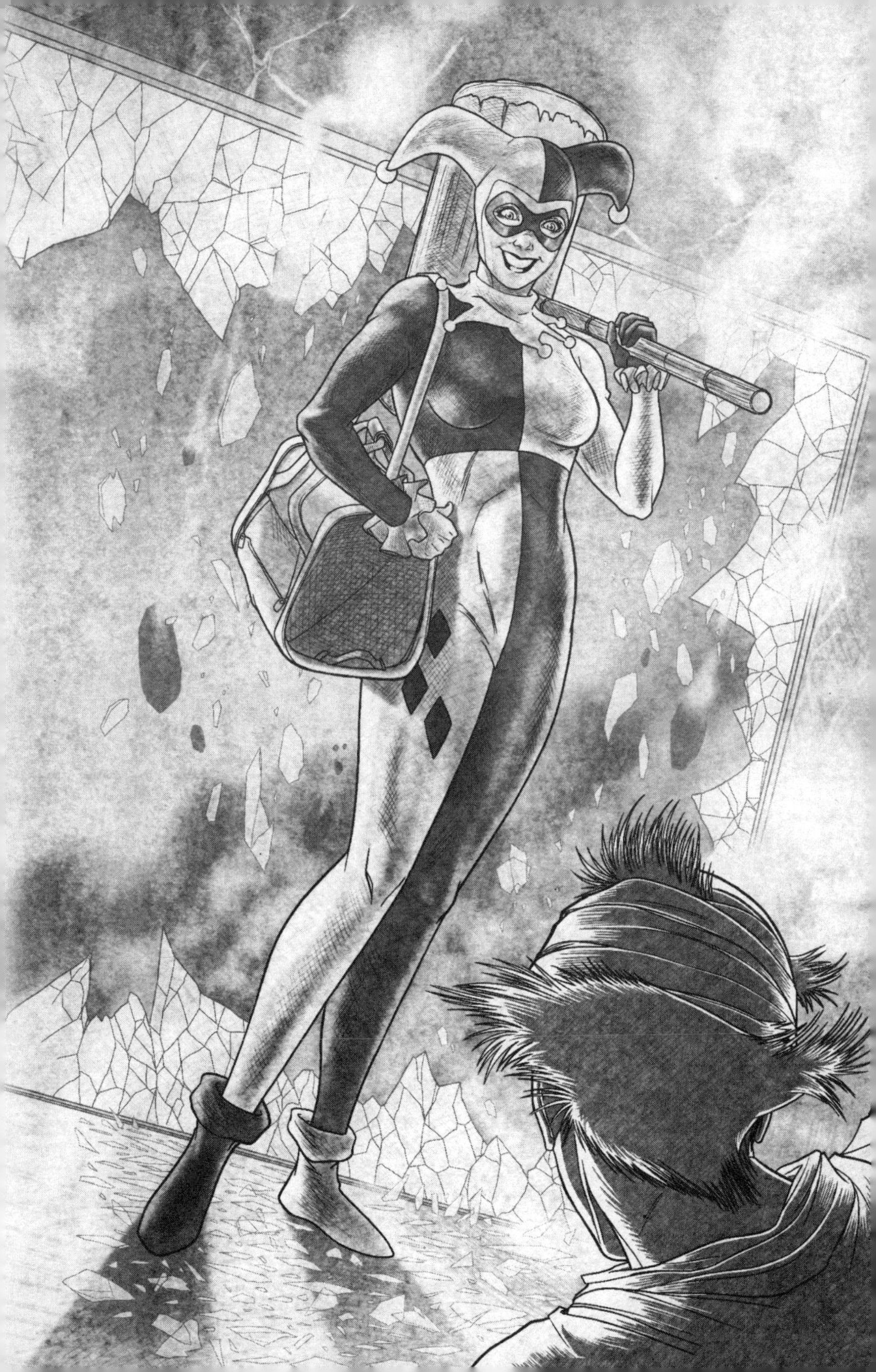

"So," she said as she stepped closer to him, "whaddaya think? Say hello to your new, improved HARLEY QUINN!"

The Joker grinned. "Well, I'll tell you. You look a bit like my inmate friend, and you look a bit like my therapist." Harley's face froze. "But," he continued, "you look like a lot more fun than either of them! Whaddaya say we get out of here?"

"Puddin'," Harley replied, "I thought you'd never ask!"

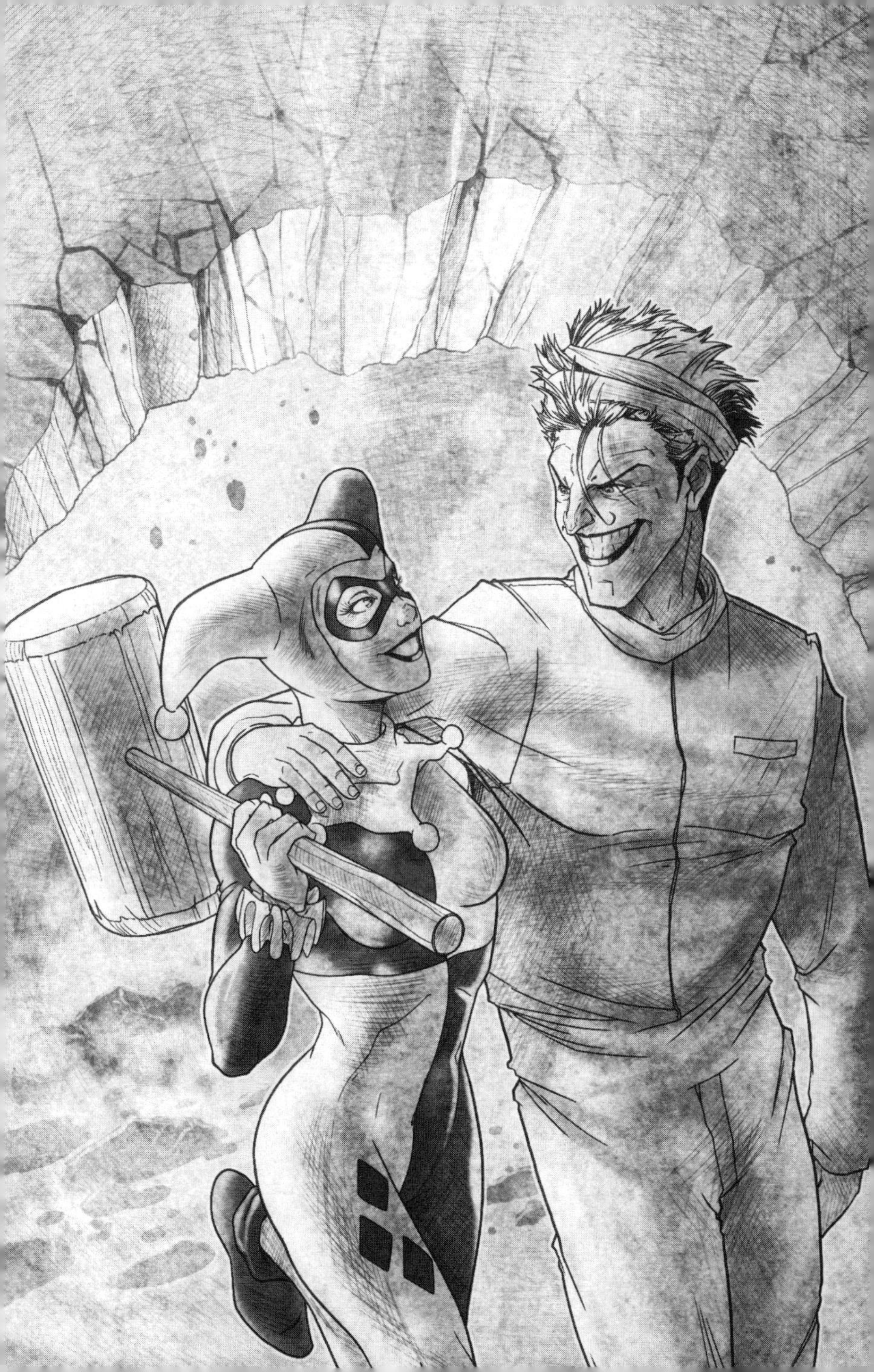

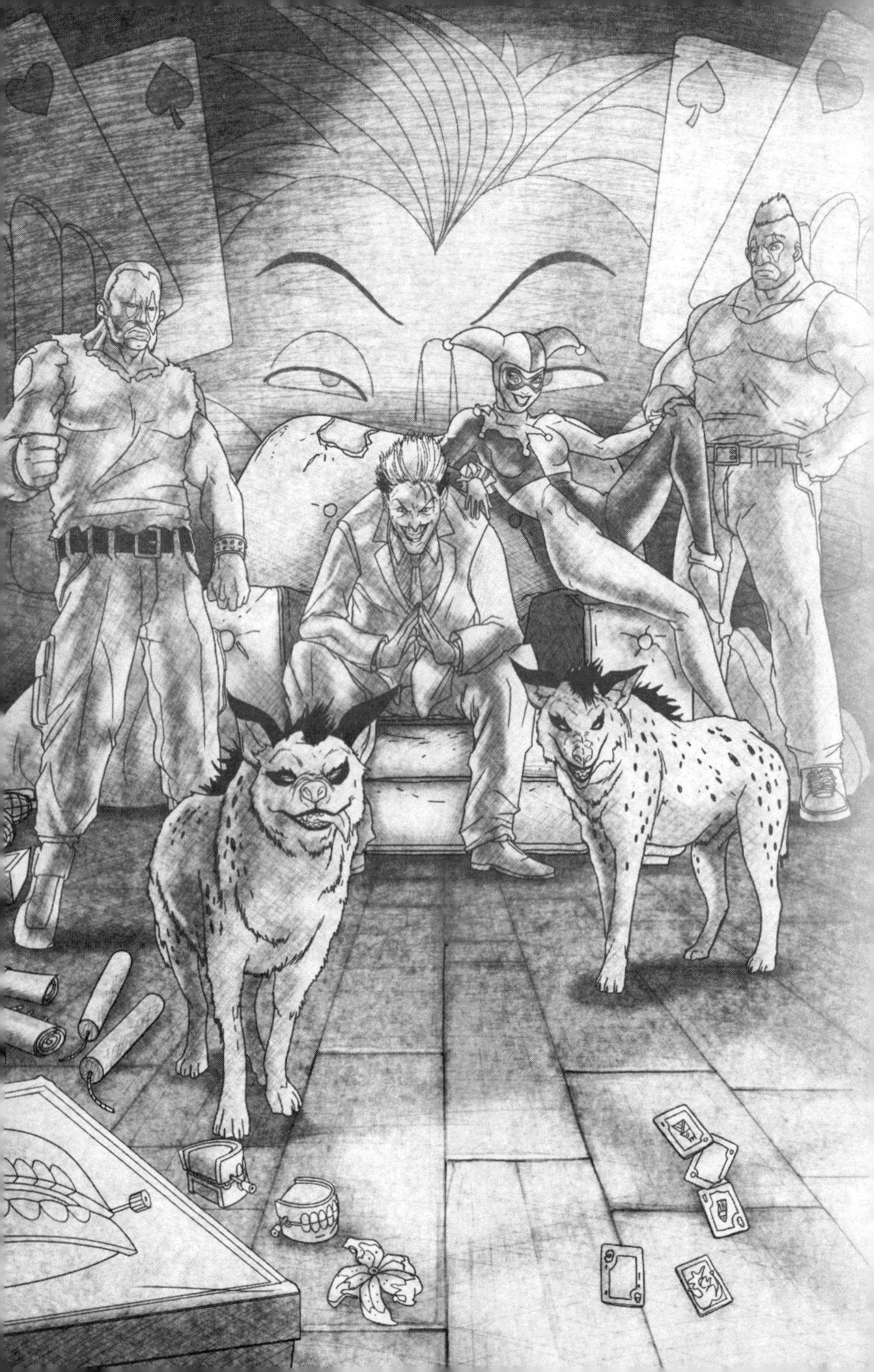

CHAPTER FOUR

AVERSION THERAPY

Harley quickly settled into her new life as the Joker's girlfriend, and at first everything was wonderful. They spent their days in one of the Joker's many hideouts, dreaming of new capers and pranks to pull on Gotham City. They spent their nights out on the town with the Joker's hired gang members, committing crimes and making mischief. She and the Joker even adopted two hyenas and named them Bud and Lou, and Harley loved talking to and playing with her "babies." Every day was full

of laughter and loot. They were well on their way to being a happy criminal family.

But more and more, the Joker got angry when

You knew there was a "But" coming, Right? I Don't have a lot to say about this part. Just Trust me, I figure it out Eventually.

Batman and his sidekick Robin would foil their plans. The Joker used to think that running from Batman was all part of the fun, but now he was

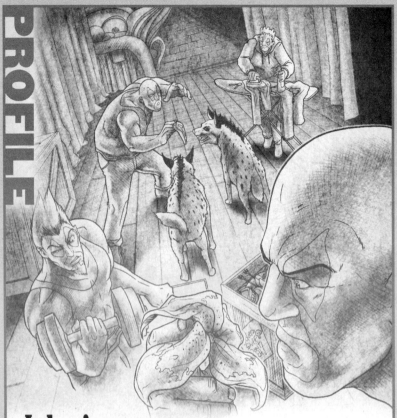

Joker's gang

The Joker likes having an audience, which means that he usually has a gang around to keep him company. There are always ambitious young criminals in Gotham City, looking to make a name for themselves, and joining the Joker's gang can seem like a good way to begin their lawbreaking career. To be in the Joker's gang, though, they have to be able to "take a joke," which includes everything from "being first through the door during a robbery" to "being the first to test the new batch of toxic laughing gas." As a result, the Joker is usually looking for new gang members.

talking as if it spoiled the joke. And if there one was one thing Joker hated, it was having one of his jokes spoiled.

Harley wanted the best for him, and she tried to help. But often it seemed like everything she did was wrong. When she made a suggestion, the Joker would yell that it was the dumbest idea he had ever heard. When she kept quiet, the Joker would claim that she wasn't pulling her weight in the gang.

Harley had an idea: If she got rid of Batman, she would prove that she was a useful part of the gang, and they wouldn't have to worry about Batman anymore! And to show the Joker that his ideas were as great as they always had been, she would use one of his plans to do it!

Harley found the perfect plan to use. At one point, the Joker had been thinking of building a trap he called "The Death of a Hundred Smiles." Batman would fall through a trap door into a tank full of deadly, meat-eating fish called piranhas. The

55

last thing the Joker wanted Batman to see before he died was all the hungry piranhas smiling their toothy grins at him. When the Joker realized that piranhas can't smile, and, in fact, they usually look like they're frowning, he had discarded the plan in frustration.

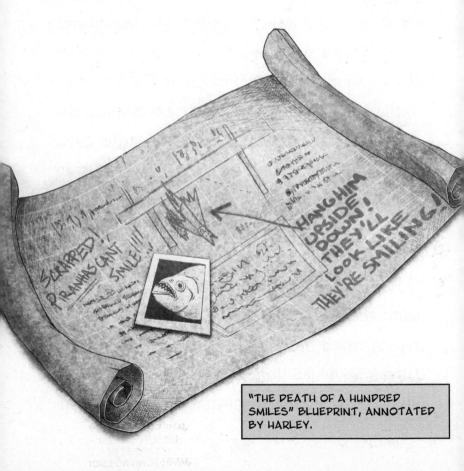

"THE DEATH OF A HUNDRED SMILES" BLUEPRINT, ANNOTATED BY HARLEY.

But Harley knew just how to fix it. All she had to do was lower Batman into the tank headfirst, and all those little toothy frowns would be turned upside down. It would look to him like the piranhas were smiling! She got to work right away.

First, she built everything she needed in an old warehouse. Then, she tricked Batman into meeting with her alone, and she managed to knock him out. She dragged him to the warehouse and strung him up over the tank. Now all that was left was to show the Joker her handiwork, and then they could lower Batman into the tank together. He was going to love it!

Except, he didn't love it. He *hated* it. He hated that Harley had come up with a way to fix his plan that he hadn't thought of, and he *especially* hated that Harley had been the one to catch Batman. In the Joker's mind, if anyone besides him caught the Batman, that would completely and utterly ruin the joke. He yelled at Harley for so long and so loudly that Batman woke up and was able to escape.

That made the Joker even angrier, and from then on their relationship was even worse. Anything that

went right the Joker took all the credit for. Anything that went badly he blamed on Harley.

One day, after a routine heist went wrong, he declared that Harley was useless to him. He shouted that he didn't want to see her around anymore, and he kicked her out of the gang!

Harley was hurt, embarrassed, and angry. She decided to try to prove herself yet again, but this time she would do it all on her own. When the Joker saw what a good criminal she was without him, she thought, surely he'd change his mind and take her back.

Soon enough, her opportunity came along. The Gotham Museum of Natural History was displaying the gorgeous Harlequin Diamond for a limited time only—how could she resist stealing that? She knew the crime had to be perfect, so she planned for everything.

At least, she thought she did. She quietly cut her way into an unguarded skylight and lowered herself on a cable into the gallery where the diamond was being displayed. To avoid setting off the security alarms, she used a smoke bomb to show her where the laser trip wires were. Then she vaulted and somersaulted and shimmied her way past the lasers until she was right next to the diamond. Just one more second, and she would have it.

Suddenly, all the lights came on and the alarms started blaring! What could have gone wrong?

Look at me go!
WHEEEEEEEE!

Harley grabbed the diamond and ran out of the gallery toward the nearest exit. She raced around a corner and ran right into . . . Poison Ivy!

Ivy had escaped from Arkham and was stealing some rare plant toxins from the museum's botanical collection. Ivy was the one who had set off the alarms! Harley was annoyed at having her perfect crime spoiled. But when the police showed up at the museum, she realized that she and Ivy could work

together to escape. She loaded some of the plant toxins into one of her smoke bombs and tossed it at the cops, causing them to cough uncontrollably. Then Harley and Ivy ran out to Ivy's car and drove off together.

Ivy was impressed with Harley's quick thinking. As they sped toward Ivy's hideout, she told Harley, "This could be the beginning of a beautiful friendship."

Ivy was absolutely right. But before she and Harley could spend more time together, Ivy had to make sure that she didn't accidentally poison her new friend. That night in Ivy's hideout near a toxic waste dump, she injected Harley with a serum that would make her immune to the toxins in Ivy's blood . . . and for that matter all the chemicals that were lying around the hideout! Harley was touched, and Ivy reminded her what Harley had said to her when they first met: "Friendships should be built on a strong foundation of trust." She also invited Harley

Poison Ivy

Dr. Pamela Isley has always been more fond of plants than of people. While she was working on some new plant-derived poisons as part of her biochemistry research, there was an accident in her lab. The toxic chemicals spilled all over her! But instead of killing her, they gave her the ability to control plants with her mind, including encouraging them to grow to monstrous sizes. She could also control the toxins in her bloodstream and release them from her skin, allowing her to hypnotize or poison people. She committed several crimes using her new powers and was caught and sent to Arkham, but she escaped after an admirer sent her a leaf in the mail. She instructed the leaf to grow into a gigantic vine, which broke through the outside-facing window in her cell and carried her to freedom.

THIS ONE'S ON ME, TOO! WAY TO WORK THE SYSTEM, RED!

HA! NOW I SEE WHY THEY DIDN'T LET HER GET MAIL BEFORE!

Lifted this from the cop's pocket. You gotta remember the day that your best friend decides to never poison you!

EVIDENCE OF A SERUM THAT PROTECTS AGAINST POISON IVY'S TOXINS. COLLECTED FROM IVY'S LAIR BY POLICE; LOST BEFORE IT COULD BE OFFICIALLY LOGGED.

to stay with her for a while, hoping that this would help Harley realize that the Joker was no good for her.

The next few weeks were fantastic for both of them. Ivy planned robberies at places like snooty men-only clubs to help Harley get her self-esteem back. Harley appreciated her new friend looking out for her, and often told her, "Red, I like your style." And, with the two of them working together,

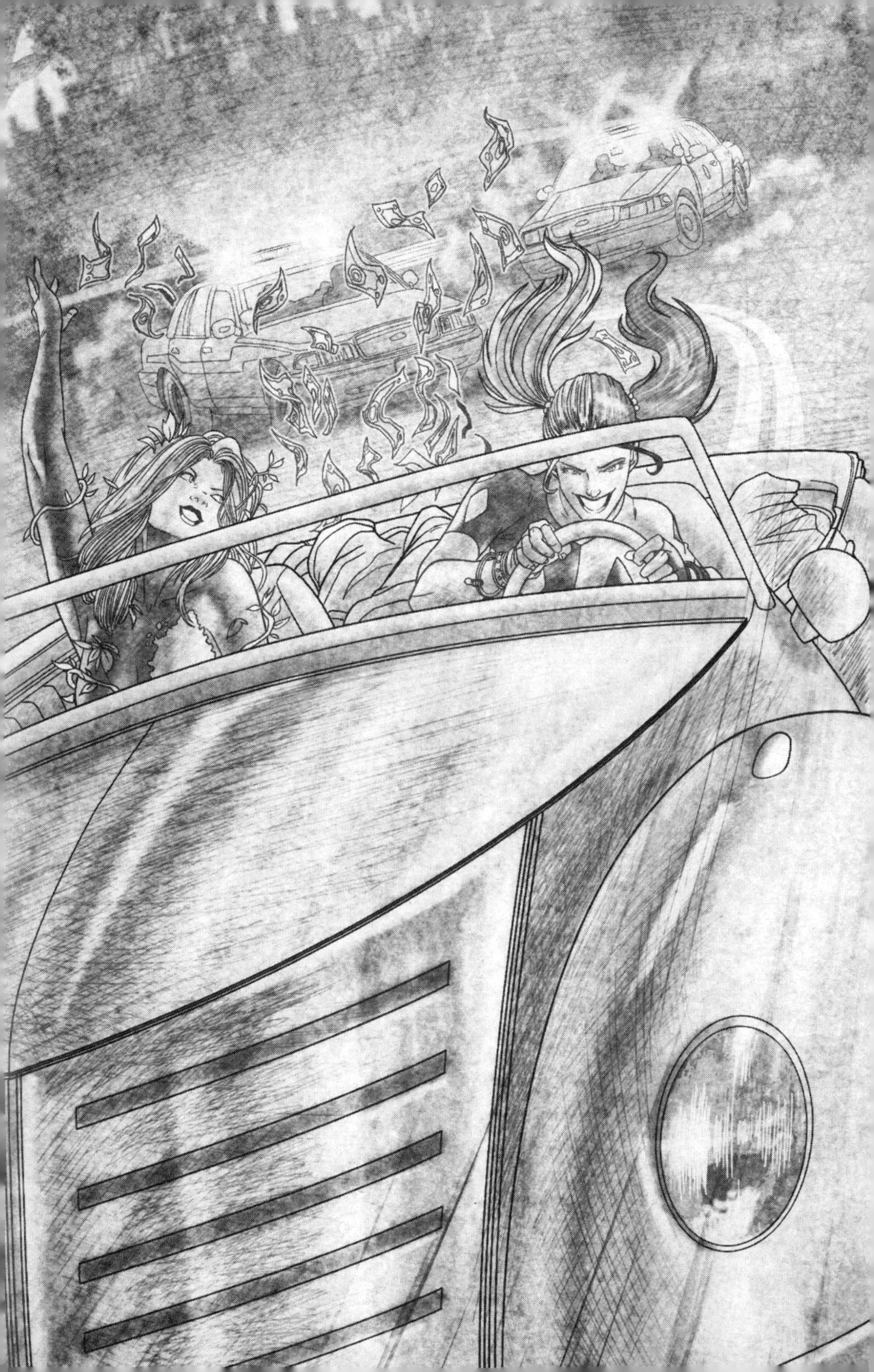

the robberies were so successful that soon the papers were calling the duo "The New Queens of Crime."

But Harley still missed the Joker. One night, when Ivy was asleep, she snuck to the phone and called him. When he picked up, she was so happy to hear his voice. "I just wanted to let you know that I'm doing all right," she told him. "How are you?"

Well, the Joker was doing terribly. Without Harley around, the hyenas weren't getting fed, everything was a mess, and no one was telling him good jokes anymore. Not only that, but he had seen the headlines in the paper about Harley and Ivy. He was furious and jealous of their success. But he would never admit any of that to her! He pretended everything was fine, and in the meantime he traced her call and discovered where she was staying.

Later that night, Harley heard a noise. She went out to the living room and found the Joker there! At first, she was thrilled, because she thought he had come to visit her. But then she noticed what he was doing: gathering up all of the loot from her robberies. He had come to steal from her!

She shouted to wake up Ivy, and the two of them faced off against the Joker. But there was no time for a fight: the Joker had told the cops where Harley and Ivy were hiding. Gotham City police soon swarmed the hideout—and Batman was with them! The Joker had planned to be long gone by the time anyone else showed up. So as soon as he heard police sirens, he dived out a window. He noticed some barrels of toxic waste near the house and fired a gun into one of them as he ran by. It exploded! The fire spread, and as other nearby barrels exploded, chunks of hot metal and rock blocked off any way for Batman and the cops to get to him. The Joker could watch with satisfaction as Harley and Ivy were caught and taken away.

Harley was devastated. How could her sweet Joker have done this to her? Especially after all she'd done to prove herself to him?

Maybe Red was right, she thought, as Batman handcuffed her. *Maybe Mr. J's not so fun after all.*

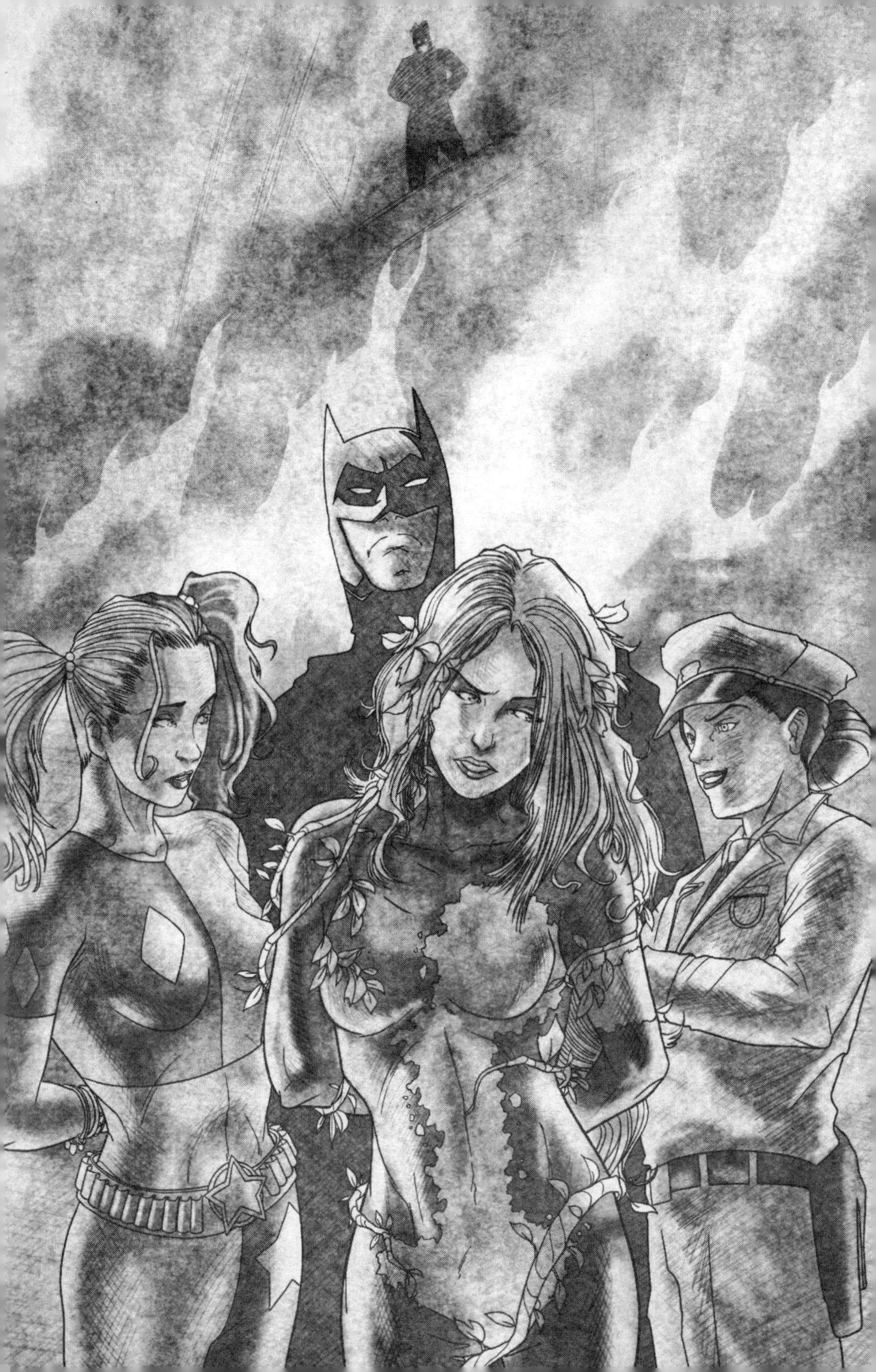

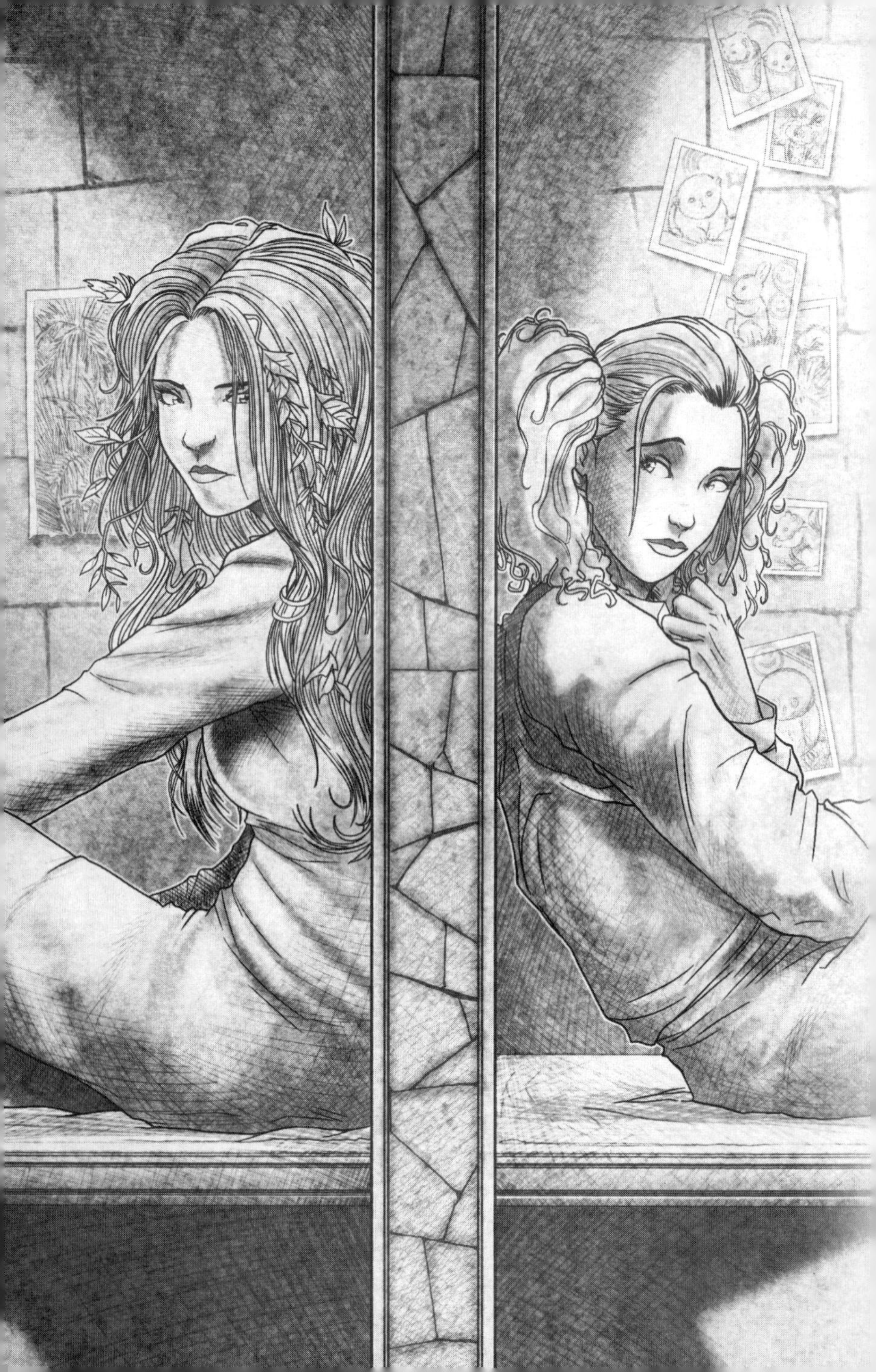

CHAPTER FIVE

SEPARATION ANXIETY

Harley didn't go to prison. Her abrupt personality shift from doctor to criminal—plus her association with other super-villains like the Joker and Poison Ivy—made the authorities think that she could use some psychiatric care. So she ended up in a familiar place: Arkham Asylum. Only this time she was one of the inmates!

Dr. Leland, once Harley's boss, wanted to see her former employee get better, so she took her on as one of her own patients. Day after day, they sat in

Dr. Leland's office and talked. Mostly they talked about the Joker, and how confused Harley was by his behavior.

Harley also talked to Ivy, who had the cell next to hers at Arkham. Ivy quickly forgave Harley for having led the Joker right to their hideout. She could see how badly Harley needed a friend to be honest with her. Between Ivy and Dr. Leland, Harley heard plenty about how the Joker had manipulated her, how selfish he was, and how she was better off without him.

NOTE RECOVERED FROM HARLEY'S CELL IN ARKHAM.

Sometimes she believed them. But sometimes she remembered how great the Joker was in the beginning, and all she wanted to do was get back to where they started.

After months, Harley seemed to be making real progress. Both Dr. Leland and Ivy were starting to believe that she was actually done with the Joker.

Then one evening, Batman showed up in Harley's cell at Arkham. He explained that the Joker, still on the loose, had gotten his hands on a bomb big enough to blow up the entire city. No one had any idea when the bomb would go off, so Batman needed to move as fast as possible to find it. He needed someone on his side who could help him find the Joker . . . who could *think* like the Joker. He needed Harley, and Dr. Leland was going to let Harley out of Arkham for the night if she would agree to help.

"No way, Batman!" Harley cried when he told her. "You think I'm going to help you, after all the trouble you caused between me and Mr. J?"

SEE? I was still Trying to Blame it on Batman! Don't worry, I get it Pretty soon now.

Gotham City

Gotham City has always been a city in conflict. Crime has deep roots there, and sometimes even the police or city officials take bribes from one of the city's many criminal organizations. Because of this, Gotham City is an attractive destination for super-villains, and the citizens of Gotham are often in danger. Batman, Robin, and their allies battle tirelessly to keep their city as safe as possible, and to keep the villains in prison or in Arkham Asylum, where they belong.

"Harley," Batman said, trying to be patient, "he could kill millions of people tonight. Can you really sit there and let that happen?"

"You don't get it, Batman," said Harley, crossing her arms and looking away. "This is just another one of his jokes. He would never flatten Gotham City. For one thing, *I'm* in Gotham City!"

"What makes you think he cares about that? You know he wouldn't hesitate to hurt you. And not just you: What about your friends, like Ivy? What about your hyenas?"

That got Harley's attention. "Red? And the babies? You think Mr. J would blow up *the babies*?!?

That rat! You're right, we have to stop him!"

Soon, Harley and Batman were in the Batmobile, on their way to the Joker's nearest hideout. But there was no one there! They tried another hideout, but it was also deserted.

Back in the Batmobile, Harley was getting antsy—Batman wouldn't let her push any of the buttons, and there were *so many buttons*—and Batman was getting frustrated.

"Look, Batman," Harley finally said. "If you're so worried about Gotham City, why not get all the people out?"

"I'd love to, Harley," replied Batman, "but the mayor has to give that order, and for some reason he won't listen to me. I called him at his house and he refused to evacuate the city."

Harley burst out laughing. "Oh, nice one, Mr. J!" she giggled.

Batman stared at her.

"Think about it, Batman!" Harley said. "What better way to tie up the city . . . than to tie up the mayor?!"

Batman understood immediately and called Robin. "Robin, meet me at the mayor's house right away! The Joker has the mayor hostage!"

When they got to the mayor's house, they found some of the Joker's henchmen loading the bomb into a plane, while the Joker lounged by the mayor's pool, twirling a weapon around his finger. Bobbing on an inflatable duck in the middle of the pool was the mayor, wrapped from his chest to his ankles in rope and completely helpless.

Harley overheard the Joker bragging to the mayor about his plan. Batman had been right. The Joker really was planning on blowing up the whole city, including her, her friends, and the hyenas! That was the last straw: She and Mr. J were officially through.

TA-DAAAAAAAAAA! TOLD YA

PART OF THE FLOATIE FROM THE MAYOR'S POOL, KEPT BY HARLEY AS A MEMENTO.

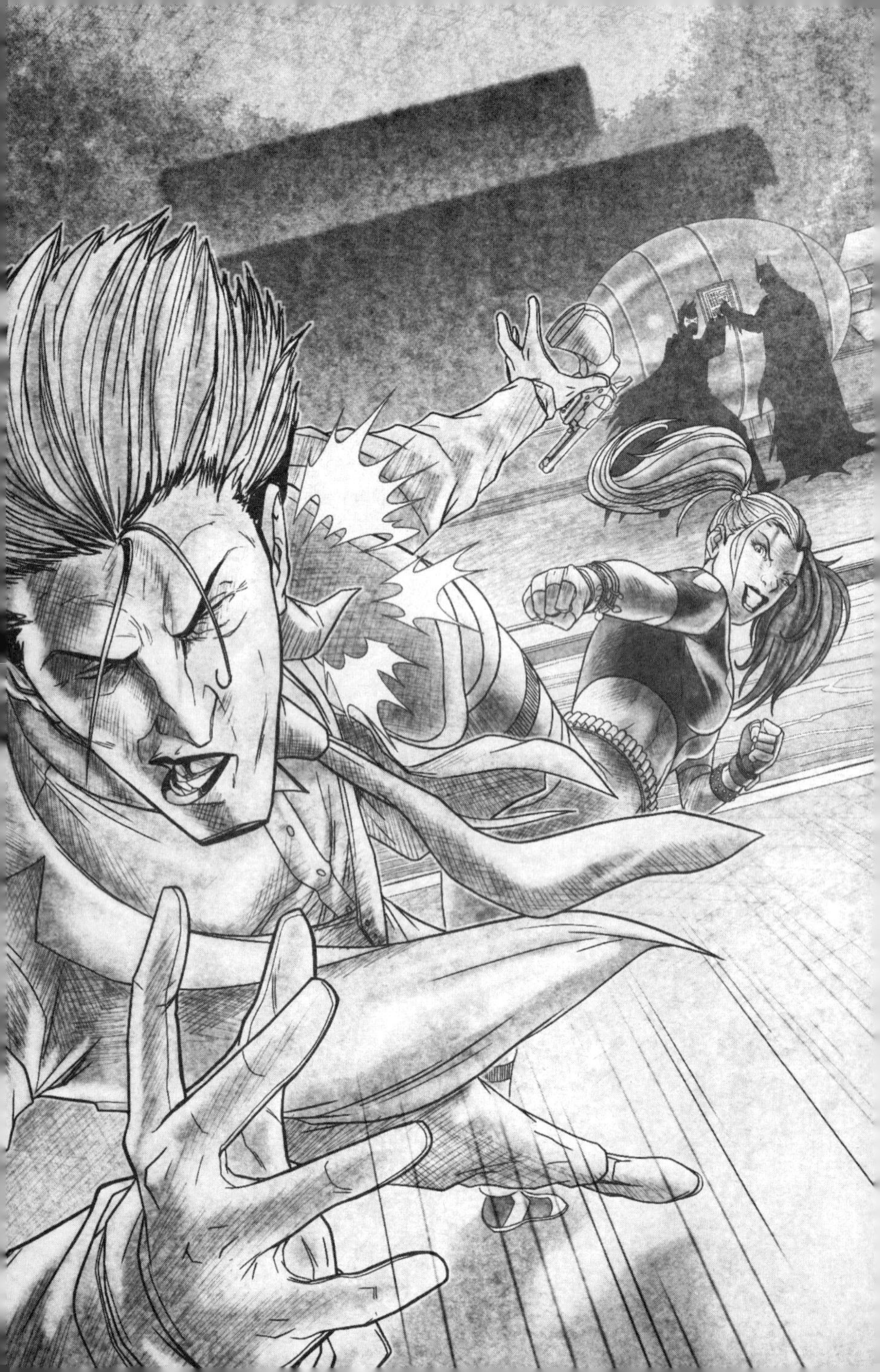

Batman and Robin had told her to wait while they quietly knocked out the henchmen, defused the bomb, and rescued the mayor. But she was in no mood to wait. She ran out and took on the Joker by herself. She was so angry, and he was so startled, that she had no trouble knocking him down and taking his weapon.

As Batman and Robin put the Joker in the back of the Batmobile, Harley realized the irony of what was happening. She had just officially given up on the Joker. And yet here she was, being handed exactly what she had wanted for months: She and the Joker were going right back to where they had started. They were headed back to Arkham together!

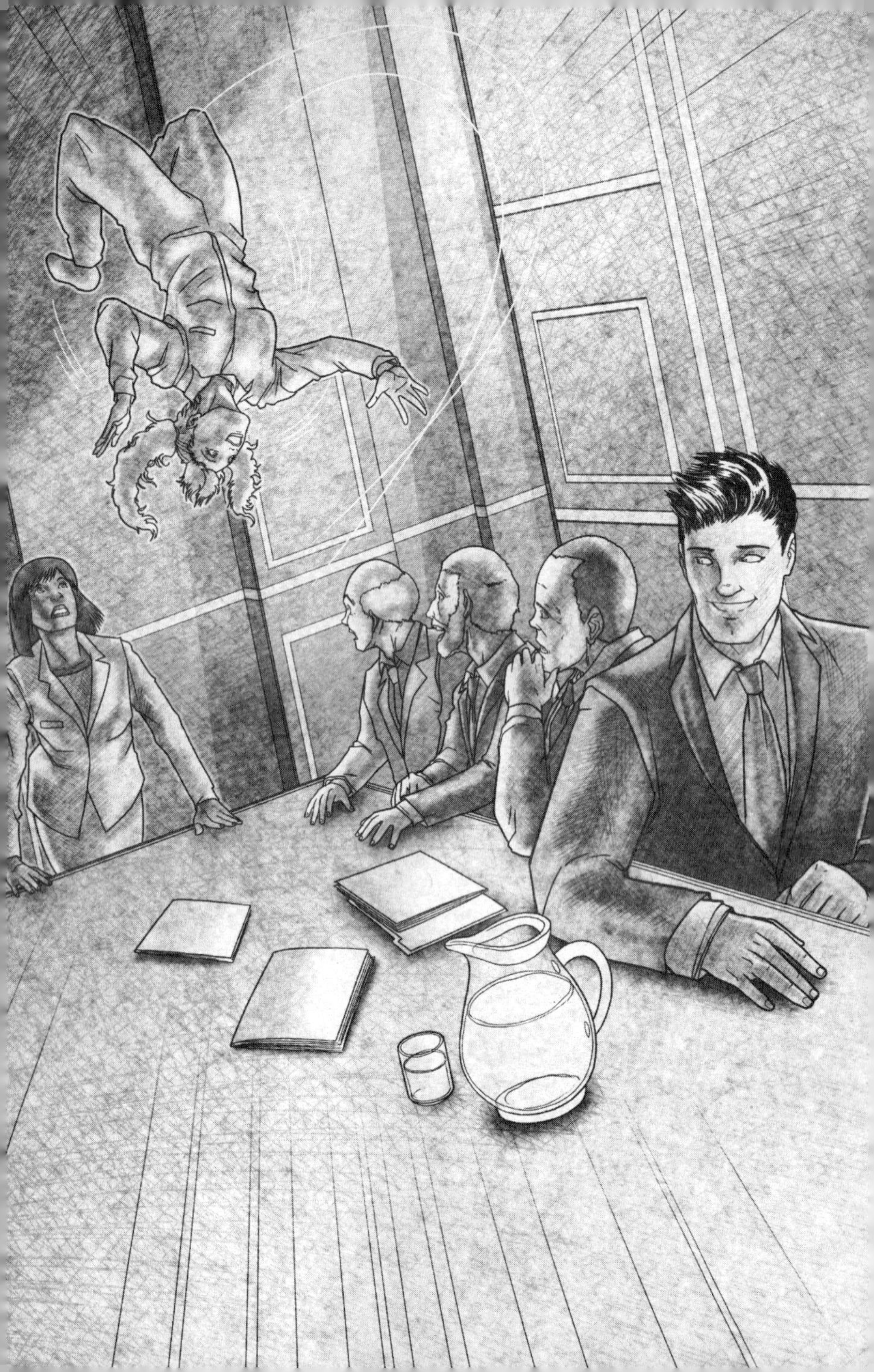

CHAPTER SIX

INTERVENTIONS

Happily, Harley didn't have to stay in Arkham for much longer. Dr. Leland was very impressed with how Harley had helped Batman and Robin save Gotham City, especially since she had to fight the Joker to do it. So Dr. Leland called a special meeting of Arkham's executive board. In some situations, the board had the power to shorten an inmate's sentence and free them early.

In the meeting, Harley sat nervously in front of a table full of doctors and other board members, trying

Bruce Wayne

After witnessing the murder of his parents when he was just a child, Bruce Wayne dedicated his life to fighting crime and making Gotham City a better place. Using his huge fortune and the power of his company, Wayne Enterprises, Bruce invests in countless charities and worthy causes. He is very interested in criminals who want to turn their lives around, and he has donated enough money to Arkham Asylum that he has been granted a seat on the asylum's executive board.

to answer their questions honestly. At first, it didn't look good. Some of the board members weren't convinced that she should leave the asylum, and nothing Harley was saying seemed to be changing their minds.

Then a man at the end of the table spoke up. It was Bruce Wayne, and he argued that Harley was a very unusual case. Her former career helping criminals to reform should be taken into account, he said. Based on that, plus her progress in therapy and her willingness to assist in capturing the Joker, he strongly believed that she deserved to be treated as an exceptional patient.

Harley had no idea why Bruce Wayne would have faith in her, but was she ever glad he did. He and Dr. Leland managed to convince the rest of the board, and then—she couldn't believe her ears—they were telling her that she could leave!

The next day, Dr. Leland walked Harley toward the front gates of the asylum. Dr. Leland wanted to make sure Harley had a plan for staying out of trouble.

Harley had some savings left over from working at Arkham. She promised Dr. Leland she would use that money to start a new life. In fact, she was already planning to write a book—an exposé all about the Joker!

Dr. Leland thought that was a great idea. And with that, the doctor told Harley she was free to go.

"That's it?" Harley cried. "I feel like I should get . . . I don't know, a graduation certificate or something. Do you have any of those?"

"I'm afraid not."

"Well," said Harley, batting her eyes, "could you make me one?"

HEE HEE HEE. OF course I Knew she Didn't give the patients AWARDS. I Just Really WANTED ONE!

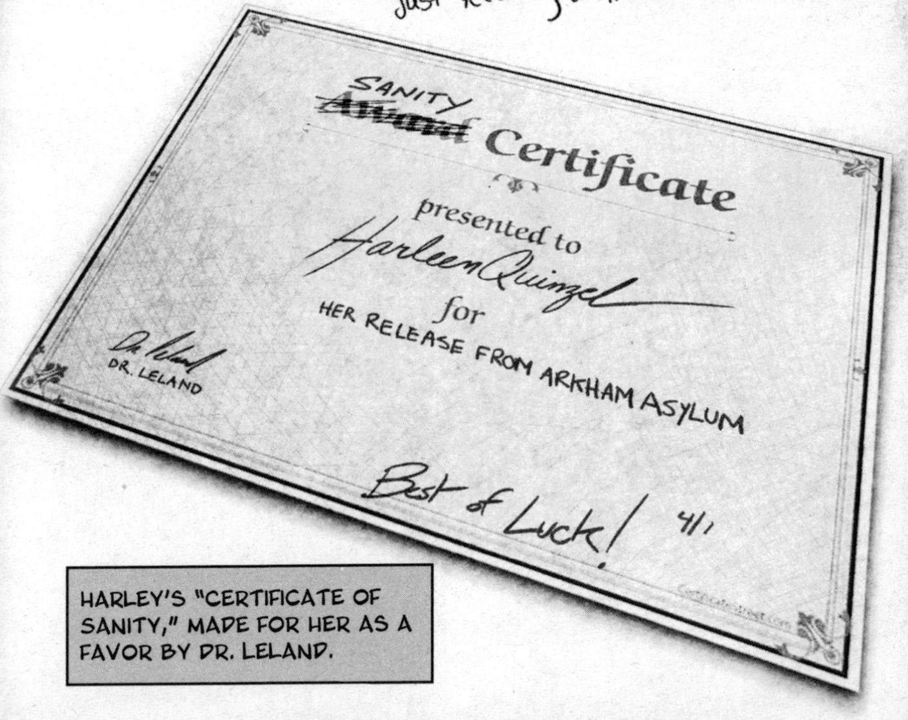

~~Award~~ SANITY Certificate
presented to
Harleen Quinzel
for
HER RELEASE FROM ARKHAM ASYLUM
Dr. Leland
DR. LELAND
Best of Luck!
4/1

HARLEY'S "CERTIFICATE OF SANITY," MADE FOR HER AS A FAVOR BY DR. LELAND.

A week later, Harley was sticking to her plan. With one little change: The first thing she did once she left Arkham was find Bud and Lou. If she was going to stay out of trouble, she needed her babies to keep her company! Then she rented a cheap room where pets were allowed, and she bought a cheaper typewriter. When she wasn't walking the hyenas,

she was working on her new book. Everything was going fine. Harley started to think that she could make this "regular life" thing work for her.

Sadly, Harley's holiday from her former life was about to end. Word had gotten around Arkham that she was writing a new book on the Joker, and the Joker was furious about it! He knew she was going to make him look bad, and he couldn't stand it. He called in all his favors with the other inmates and the guards, and he escaped Arkham again—this time inside a cart full of dirty laundry. He knew Batman and the police would be after him in no time, so he had to move fast.

That evening, Harley was typing away at her desk while the hyenas slept on the unmade bed behind her. Suddenly, the window next to her shattered! She threw her hands up to protect herself, and as soon as she lowered them she saw the Joker looming over her. He reached for the flower on his lapel and shot his toxic Joker venom at her!

But Harley was too fast for him. She vaulted out of her chair and landed on the other side of the room. The Joker venom splattered harmlessly over her desk.

"Ah ah ah, Mr. J!" she said, wagging her finger at him. "Don't forget, I know all your tricks!"

"That's exactly the problem, Harl!" the Joker growled.

Harley laughed, the hyenas growled angrily, and the fight was on.

Harley knew she had the Joker beat. He had come alone, and with her babies on her side, it was three versus one. No problem.

Suddenly, Batman and Robin came swooping into the room. Harley realized they must have tracked

Joker from Arkham. Now it was five versus one! As soon as his feet hit the floor, Batman fired a net at the Joker, and before Harley could blink the fight was over.

"Hey, Batman!" Harley complained. "I had this under control!"

Batman looked up from where he was tying the Joker's hands and feet. "I know you did, Harley," he said, "but you're supposed to be staying out of trouble, remember?"

"How can I do that when the trouble finds me?" she wailed.

For once, Batman didn't have a good answer for her.

Luckily, an old friend came to the rescue. Poison Ivy had escaped from Arkham again by ~~\~\~\~\~\~\~\~\~\~\~\~\~\~\~\~~ ~~\~~ and suggested that the two of them go to stay with another criminal known as Catwoman.

"You want us to team up with Kitty?" Harley asked. "But why?"

Hey! We can't give away All of Red's best gags!

Catwoman

Early in her career as a jewel thief, Selina Kyle decided to embrace the media calling her a "cat burglar" and transformed herself into the villain Catwoman. In addition to being a stealthy master thief, she is incredibly acrobatic and skilled in martial arts. Lately, though, she has stopped committing her trademark high-profile crimes. There are rumors that this is because she has developed a secret crush . . . on the Batman!

"We're all looking for protection right now," said Ivy, "and none of us is in the mood for big, showy heists. If we stick together, we can stay safe from the heroes and the villains."

The two of them pitched their plan to Catwoman, and she agreed. For a little while, everything went smoothly. There was only one sour note: Catwoman and Ivy insisted that Harley give the hyenas up for adoption. They argued that the wild animals were dangerous to the other pets in their new neighborhood, and Harley was forced to admit they had a good point.

Working together, they kept each other safe. They fought off henchmen that the Joker sent after Harley. They fought off crooks who thought that Catwoman was passing secret information to Batman. At Ivy's insistence, they fought villains whose plans would have damaged the environment. And they did all this while keeping off of the police's radar; they all assumed that the cops would be suspicious of anything they did.

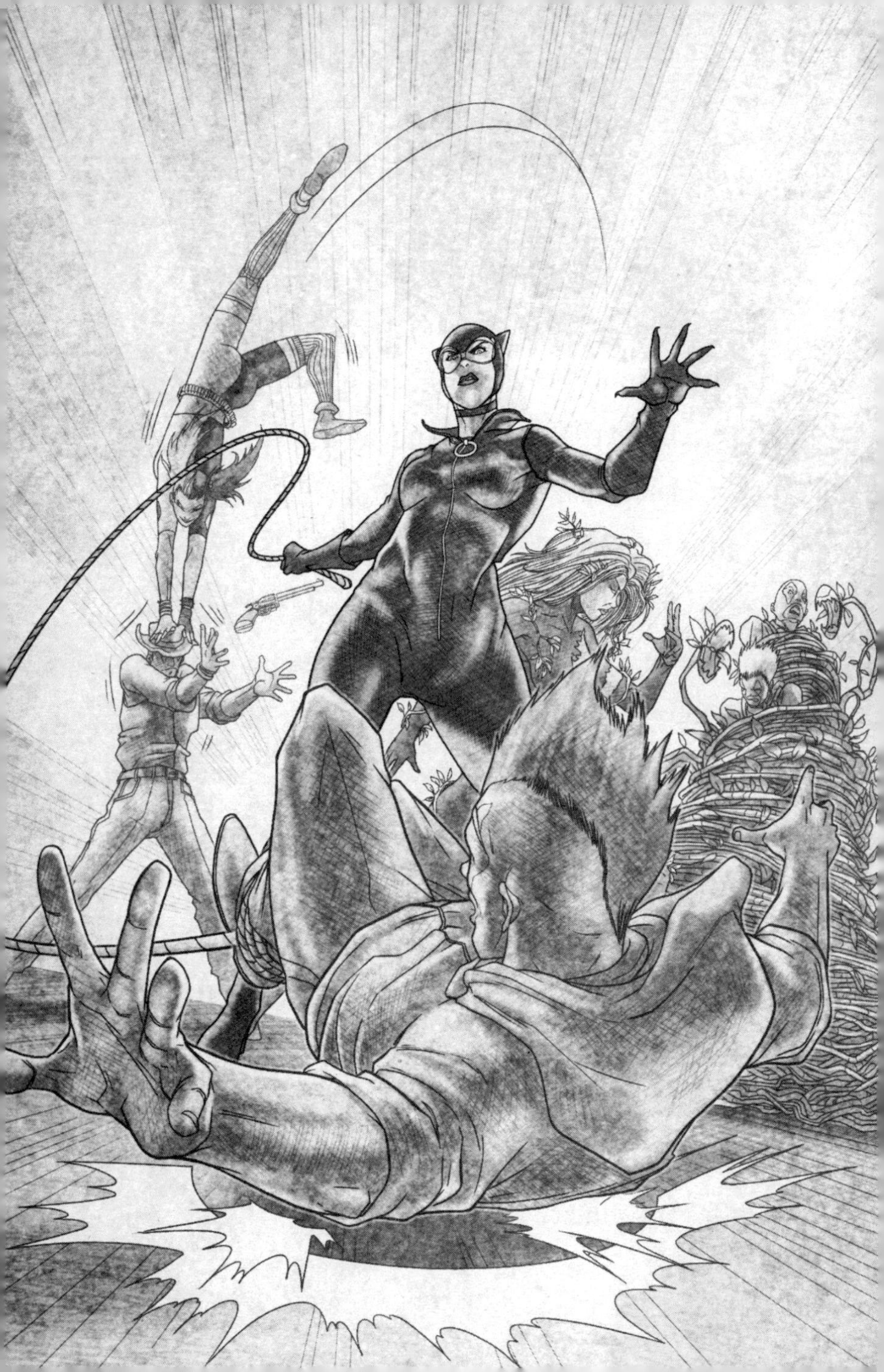

That assumption is what landed Harley in trouble again. It started small. One day, she was buying a dress in a fancy store and the clerk at the cash register forgot to remove the security tag. When Harley left the store, the alarm went off, and instead of believing that everything would be worked out fairly, Harley panicked and ran!

Running away only made things worse. Now the store thought she *had* been trying to steal something, and they called the cops. As soon as the cops realized who they were chasing, they called Batman. To get away faster, Harley stole a car, but the car had someone inside it. Harley had accidentally kidnapped a general's daughter! Now the military was involved. A car chase began that went completely out of control, ending in a huge accident involving the stolen car, a police car, a delivery truck, and a tank.

No one was seriously injured, but Harley was in a lot of trouble.

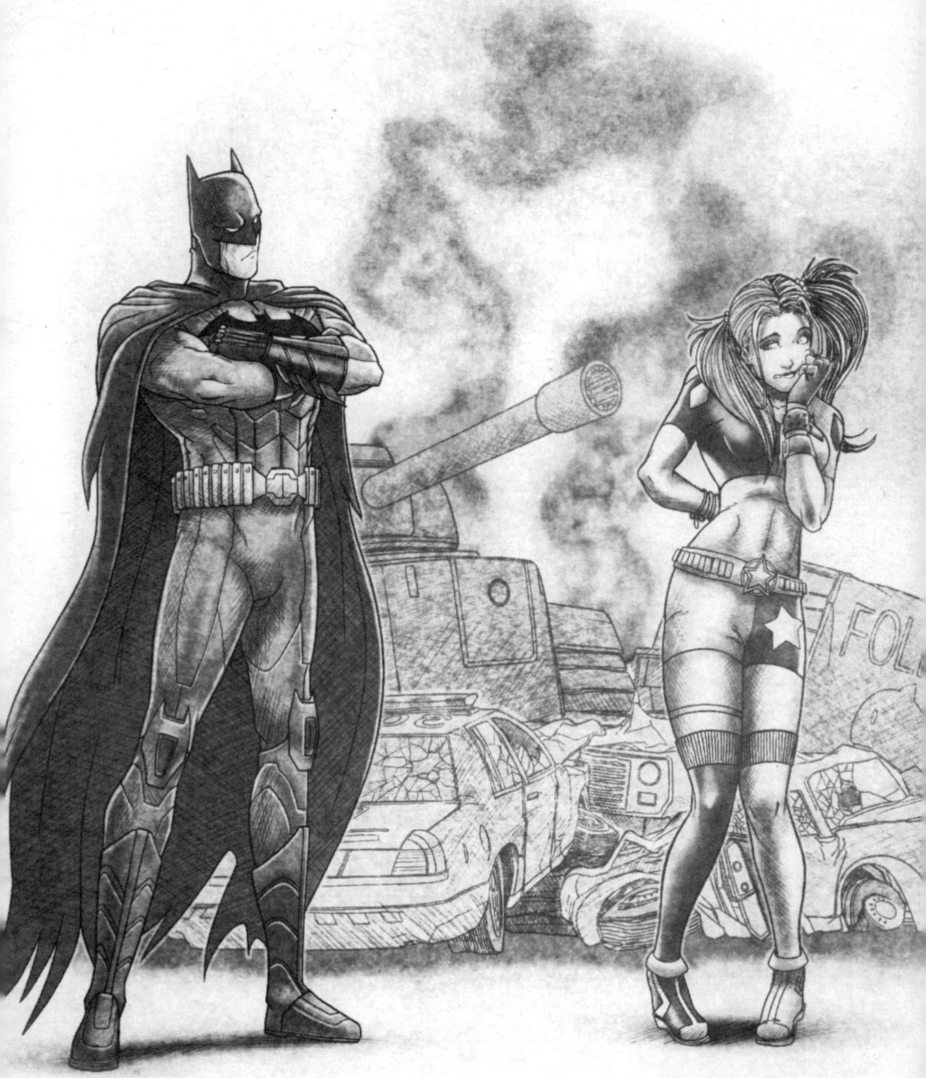

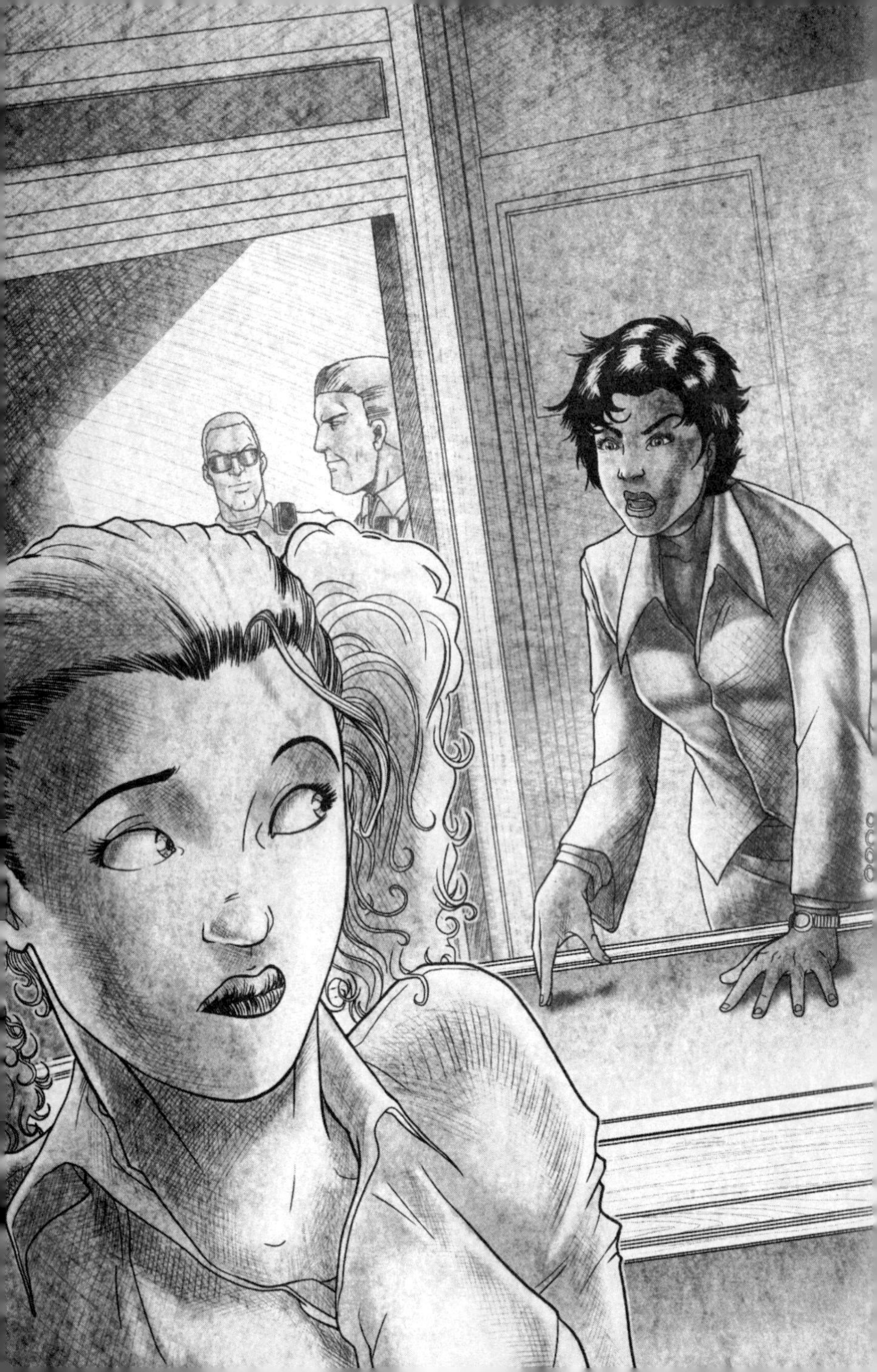

CHAPTER SEVEN

GROUP THERAPY

Harley was arrested at the scene of the accident. Since she had been legally declared sane but had committed another crime, she thought she would be sent straight to prison. But instead, when the police van stopped, Harley saw she was at some kind of government facility. She was led into an office and introduced to a woman named Amanda Waller.

"Pleased to meetcha, I'm sure," said Harley, "but . . . who are you?"

"All you need to know," Waller replied, "is that I run a very special team. If you join this team, you won't have to go to prison, and you won't have to go back to Arkham. Instead, you'll be working for me."

"Uh-huh," Harley said, "and here comes the catch!"

Waller nodded. "There are two catches. The first is that you will have a small bomb planted in your neck. If you disobey my orders or try to leave the team before I dismiss you, the bomb will go off."

Harley winced. "A-And the second catch?" she stammered.

"The team is officially called 'Task Force X,' but it's earned itself a nickname: 'The Suicide Squad.' This is because the missions I will send you on are extremely dangerous. Extremely. Dangerous."

"HA!" Harley burst out laughing, no longer nervous. "Is that all? 'Dangerous'? You know I used to hang out with Mr. J, right? This'll be a breeze! Sign me up!"

Suicide Squad

Task Force X, nicknamed "The Suicide Squad," is a secret strike team of deadly criminals who have traded their prison sentences for unquestioning service to Amanda Waller. No one on the squad knows where Waller's orders come from, and the team's missions have a bizarrely wide range of objectives and locations. Only one thing is for sure: When you're on the Suicide Squad, if you make a mistake, you die.

Which stung like the Dickens!

The next day, after the tiny bomb was put under the skin in Harley's neck, she met her new teammates. Waller explained that the Squad was always recruiting, and when a team member finished serving their time on the Squad, the bomb would be removed and they'd be free to go. For now, though, the fellow criminals on her team included Deadshot, an expert marksman; King Shark, a mysterious mutated man-shark; and Captain Boomerang, a mercenary who, true to his name, fought with a boomerang.

Almost as soon as the introductions were finished, an alarm went off, and it was time for their first mission! Without knowing where they were going to end up, the four Squad members strapped on some parachutes, grabbed their weapons, and climbed into the back of a cargo plane.

On the way, Waller sent the team their mission details. A hazardous virus had broken out at the Megadome Stadium in Mississippi. The virus didn't kill people right away, but it made them mindlessly

angry and very likely to fight each other, so the
Squad had to move fast.

Waller told them that a woman named Calby
Burns, who had been inside the stadium at the
time of the outbreak, had a cure for the virus. The

stadium had been sealed, so no one could get out and spread the virus, and no one could get in . . . except the Suicide Squad. Their mission was to find Burns and get the cure back to Waller, so it could be mass-produced and spread throughout the infected crowd. And, because everyone in the stadium could potentially be saved, the Squad was supposed to hurt as few people as possible.

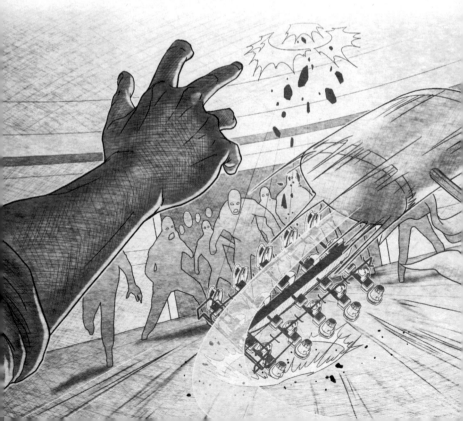

The team managed to find Calby Burns, but they were in for a surprise. The "cure" wasn't actually a cure; it was a newborn baby who was immune to the virus. A cure could be made from samples of the baby's blood, if they could just get the baby through the enraged crowds.

With Captain Boomerang carrying the baby and Harley, Deadshot, and King Shark fending off the infected people, the Squad finally made it to safety. With their help, the entire stadium full of people was saved.

After several more treacherous missions, on which Harley served willingly—Waller sometimes suspected "gleefully" was a better way to put it— Waller decided that Harley had paid for her crimes. She removed the bomb from Harley's neck and told her she was free.

But free to be . . . who? Being on the Squad had reminded Harley how much fun she could have as Harley Quinn. It also taught her she could have that fun without having anything to do with the Joker. She didn't want to go back to being Dr. Harleen Quinzel, full-time psychiatrist and author. She liked doing wacky, dangerous things, so she'd never fit in as a Super Hero. But she also liked helping people— at least, helping the people she thought deserved

it—so she didn't fit in as a villain anymore, either.
She had become Harley Quinn, Wild Card.

A CLOSE-UP OF HARLEY'S MICROBOMB
FROM HER SUICIDE SQUAD DAYS.

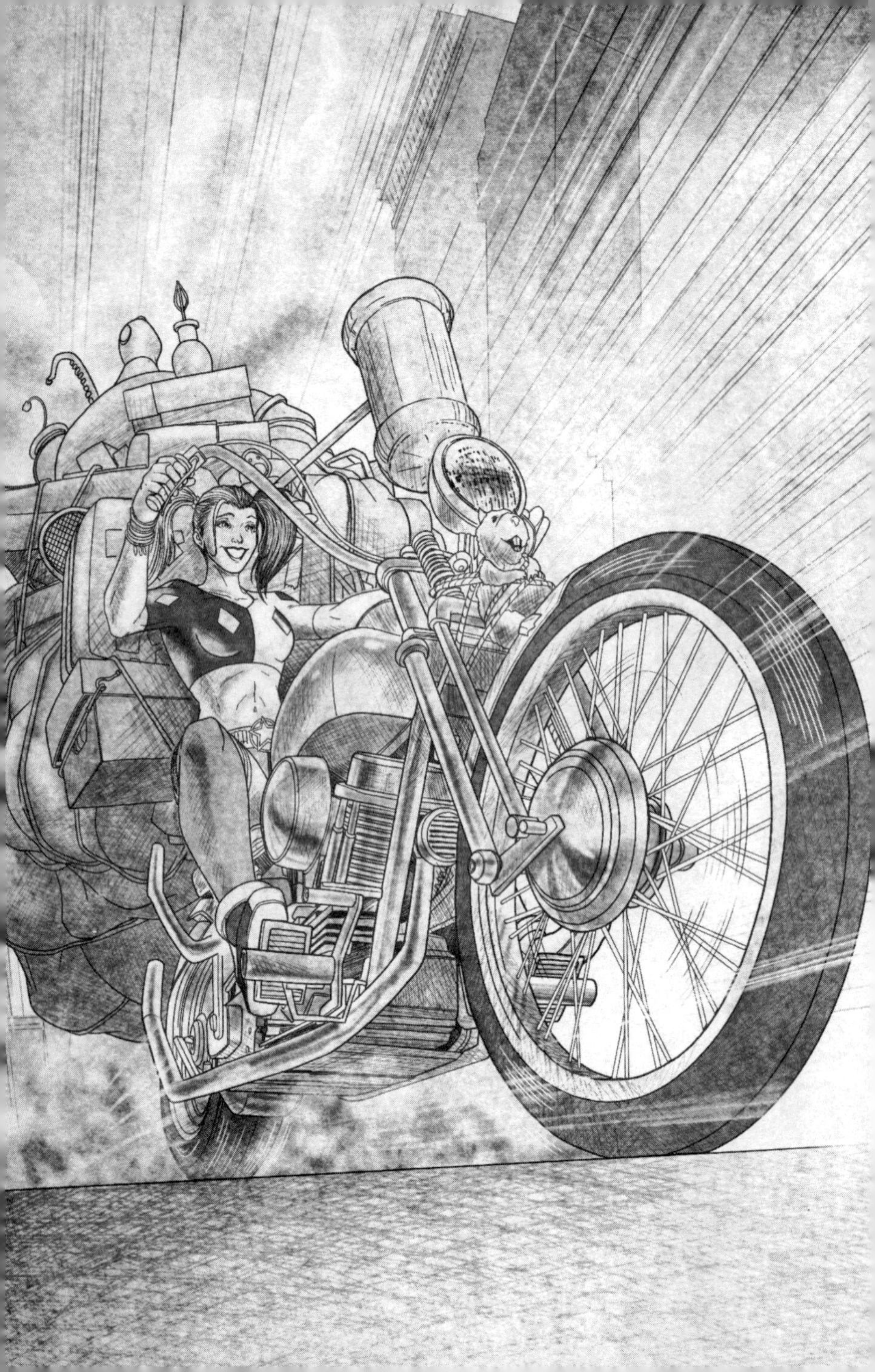

CHAPTER EIGHT

PROGNOSIS

Just when Harley realized that she wanted a fresh start, the way to do it was literally handed to her.

One day, while she was walking down the street, a big black car pulled up next to her. A man who would only say he was a lawyer handed her a letter through the car window, and then the car drove off.

Well, that was weird, Harley thought. But it was about to get weirder. The letter said that a former patient of hers, who wanted to stay anonymous,

Dear Dr. Quinzel,

I was once your patient at Arkham Asylum. You may not remember me (and I would in fact prefer that you don't), but your unusual treatment methods made a tremendous difference in my life. Based on your ideas about using my best qualities for something besides costumed crime, I was able to leave the asylum and go on to become an incredibly successful investment banker and real estate magnate.

If you are reading this, it means I have died. I have followed your career after you left Arkham with great interest, and I would like to leave you one of my Coney Island properties in my will. I fondly hope that this building will bring you great joy and help you to use your best qualities, in the same way you taught me to use mine. One of my lawyers will be in touch shortly with the details.

Forgive me for not revealing my identity to you. I changed my name after leaving the asylum and put my former life of crime entirely behind me. It is enough to say that I am,

Very sincerely yours,
A Grateful and Satisfied Client

had died and left her a four-story building in Coney Island. Harley Quinn was now a landlady!

Of course, she didn't know the first thing about being a landlady. But when had that stopped her before?

Harley fell in love with the building right away. The people who lived there, some of whom worked at a nearby freakshow, were so much fun. Plus she had so much space to herself! She quickly set about making the third and fourth floors all her own.

The third floor, which had been mostly empty and boring, went through the biggest transition. Harley heard about a nearby animal shelter that killed their pets if no one adopted them within thirty days. She was outraged. So one night, she broke into the shelter and set all the pets free so they could come live with her! But she didn't have a fun place for them to stay, so she called Poison Ivy for some help. Soon, Ivy had transformed the whole third floor into a park. The animals had never been happier.

Since Valentine's Day was coming up, before Ivy headed home, she left Harley a little present: a berry bush. A tag on the bush read, "For Finding Love."

"Aw, that was so sweet of Red!" Harley said. "And these berries smell wonderful. I wonder what they taste like?" Without another thought, she ate one.

Come on. Wouldn't you eat one?...
No? Really?

Harley's current home

Harley now owns a four-story building right near the Coney Island boardwalk. On the first floor is Madame Macabre's House of Wax and Murder, a museum showcasing wax statues of criminals. The second floor is where Harley's tenants live. The third floor was briefly used for storage, until Ivy helped Harley make it into something much more fun. And the fourth floor is all for Harley!

At first, nothing happened. But as Harley went about her day, more and more people turned their heads to look at her. She was flattered until people started to actually follow her. Then she realized: the berry was making her smell irresistible, and everyone was falling in love with her!

Soon she was sprinting down the street, trying to keep ahead of the mob of people chasing after her, yelling about how wonderful she was and how much they wanted to be with her.

She managed to get back to her apartment and lock herself inside long enough for the berry's effects

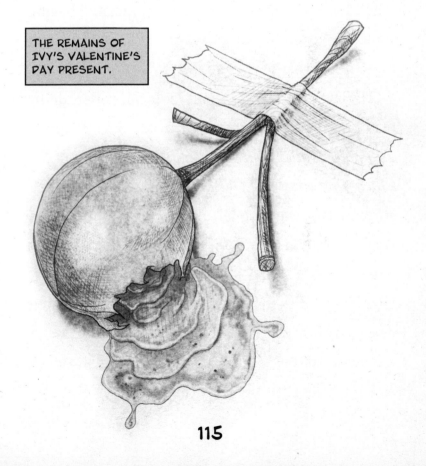

THE REMAINS OF IVY'S VALENTINE'S DAY PRESENT.

to wear off. Ivy had certainly made sure that Harley's Valentine's Day was one she would never forget!

To make some extra money, Harley took a job as a therapist in a nursing home. It was strange at first to dress up as Dr. Quinzel again, even if it was only for a few hours twice a week. But when she saw how much the residents of the home appreciated having someone listen to them, she realized she didn't mind being that person at all.

Harley also heard about a local roller derby team, and she was so excited to try out. *Zooming around on roller skates, knocking people out of the way? What's not to LOVE?* she thought. To no one's surprise, she was wonderful at it. Soon, she was the star of the Brooklyn Bruisers. And the team, which had been struggling to win matches, soon became champions in their league. They even changed their derby costumes to match hers!

Today, Harley still finds the adventures she loves, and sometimes those adventures find her. But now

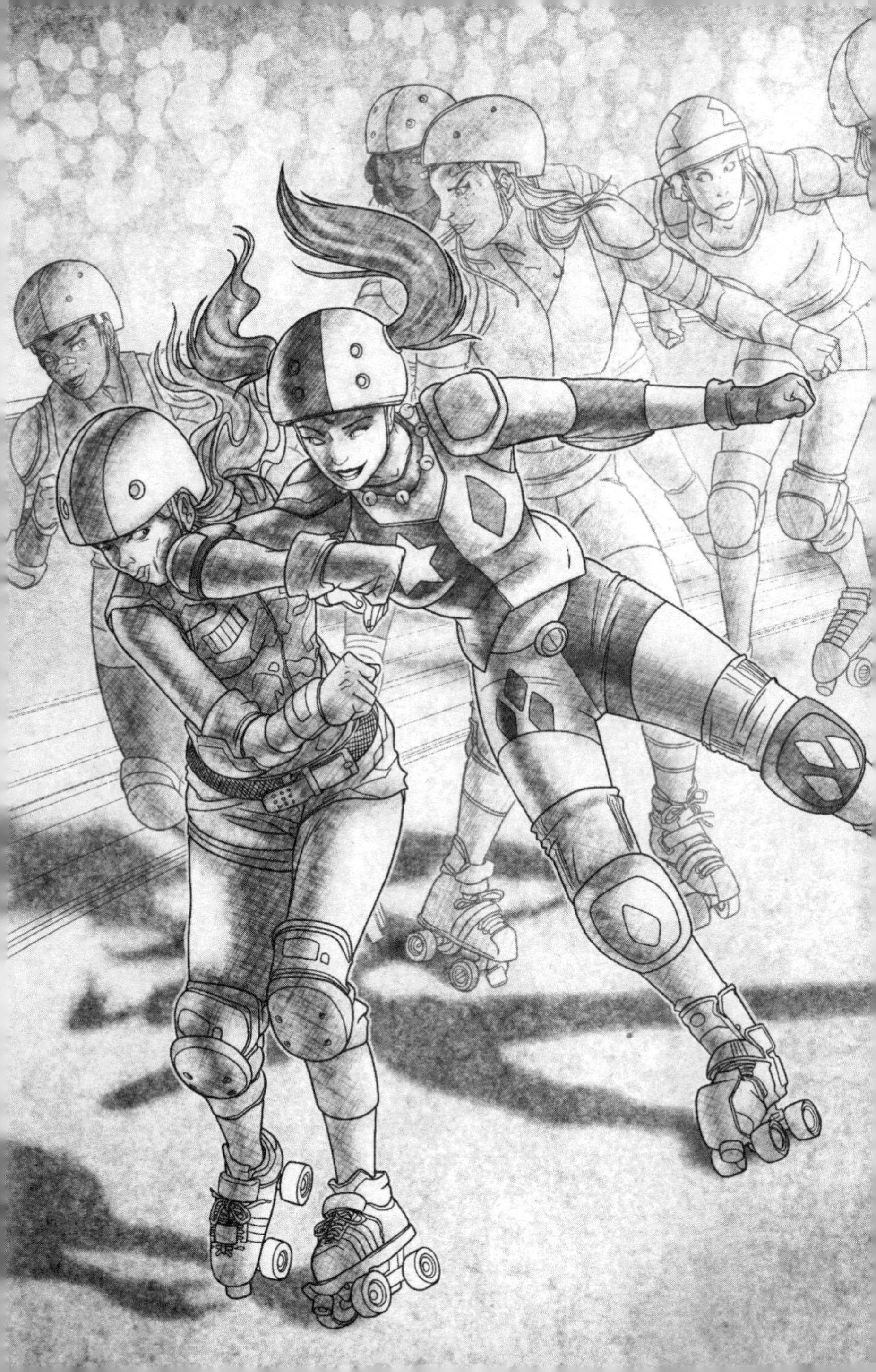

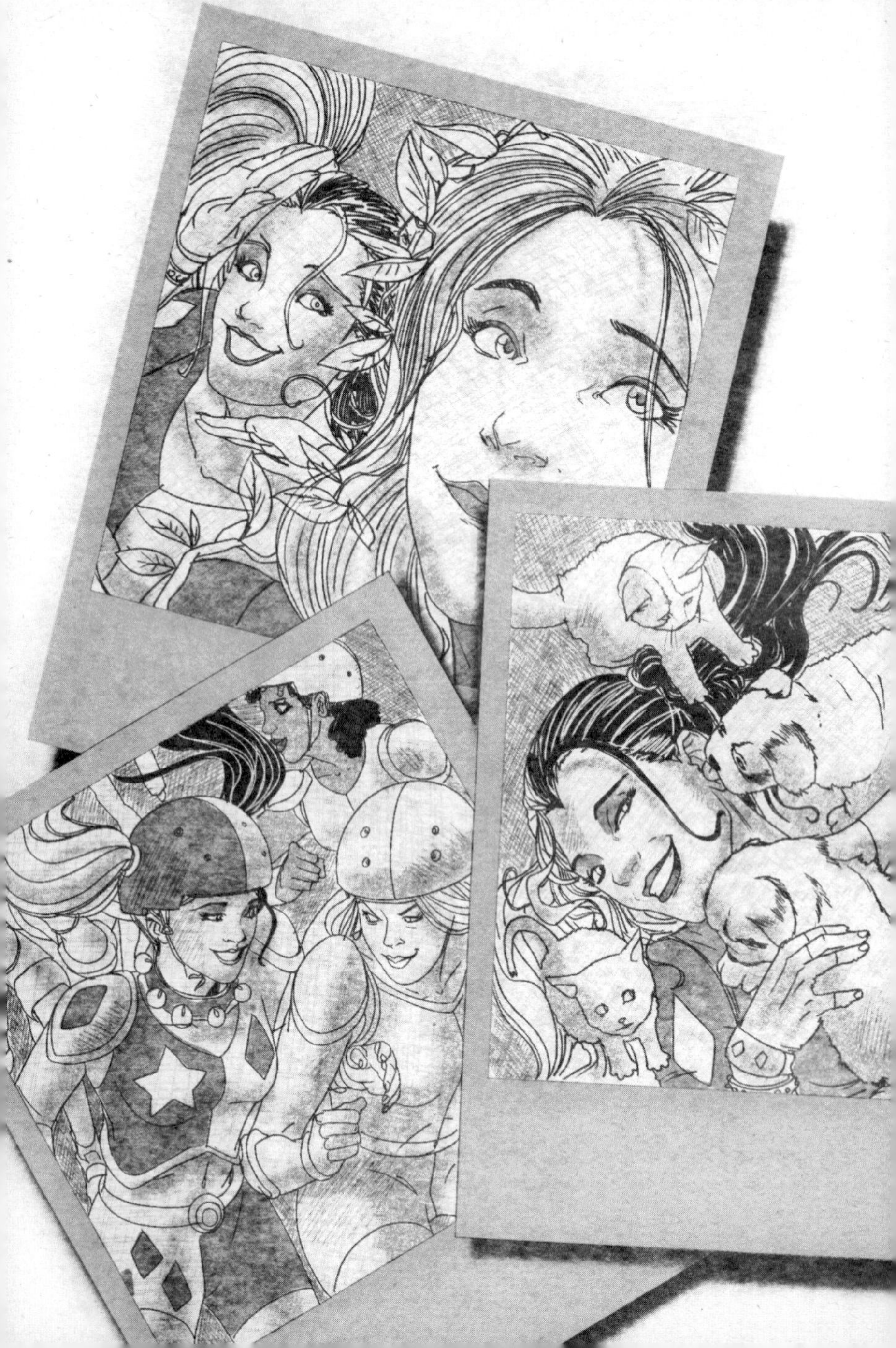

she also has friends she can count on, and she has a home and a job and a hobby to keep her grounded. She still stands out everywhere she goes. Her life is often pretty wild.

And she wouldn't want it any other way.

~~FAST~~ FACTS

◆ Harley's middle name is Frances.

◆ In college, Harley took an intelligence test for fun. She scored in the "genius" bracket.

◆ Most of Gotham's costumed criminals are sentenced to Arkham Asylum rather than regular prison.

◆ By the time the Joker met Harley, he had already been committing crimes for several years.

◆ The hyenas, Bud and Lou, liked both Harley and the Joker at first. But soon they were loyal only to Harley.

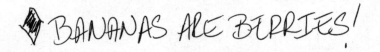 BANANAS ARE BERRIES!

- Bud and Lou are named after Bud Abbott and Lou Costello, a 1940s comedy duo.

- Harley's fighting style is based on her years of gymnastics training.

- Harley's favorite weapon is her giant mallet.

- In addition to her mallet, Harley often carries a "bag of tricks," full of smoke bombs, firecrackers, and other nasty (and usually silly) surprises.

- scientists think that on JUPITER AND SATURN IT RAINS LIQUID DIAMONDS!

- Your skin weighs About THREE TIMES AS MUCH AS YOUR BRAIN!

♦ Harley has many copies of her costume, all with different features. For instance, one version has hidden springs on the bottom of the boots for higher jumps.

♦ Harley and her best friend, Poison Ivy, have liked each other since the first time they met. At the time, Harley was Ivy's psychiatrist at Arkham.

♦ Because of the serum that Poison Ivy gave Harley, Harley is the only known person immune to Ivy's poisons.

THE BRUISERS STILL WON'T LET HARLEY USE HER MALLET DURING MATCHES.

◆ Harley had no previous roller derby experience before becoming the star player on the Brooklyn Bruisers roller derby team.

YOU CAN FIT OVER 30,000 GEESE ON A FOOtball FIELD, BUT YOU WOULDN'T WANT TO HAVE TO CLEAN UP THE FIELD Afterward.

Glossary

aversion therapy: A form of treatment in which a behavior the patient is trying to avoid (like biting her nails) is paired with something uncomfortable (like a bad taste). The patient soon thinks of the bad taste whenever she thinks of biting her nails, which makes it easier to stop the biting.

chronology: A list of events in order of when they happened.

codependency: A type of relationship where people support or encourage bad behavior in one another.

countertransference: The confusion of a therapist's feelings with that of his patient, which can sometimes lead to the therapist making wrong assumptions about a patient's motivations.

family history: A set of facts about a patient's family, gathered at the beginning of medical or psychiatric treatment, which can be useful in understanding a patient's current problems.

group therapy: A form of therapy in which a small number of people is treated together, allowing the members of the group to heal through sharing information and experiences.

harlequin: Originally a character type from Italian theater in the 1600s, the harlequin is known for her lightheartedness and agility, as well as her checkered costume.

inmate: A person who has been sentenced to stay in a prison or hospital.

intervention: When family members or friends confront a person who is ignoring a problem with his behavior, in an attempt to make that person face his problem.

novelty: A cheap toy or knickknack. More generally, anything new or unusual.

prognosis: The most likely outcome of a situation. Used in therapy to discuss how the patient will do in the future.

psychiatry: The study of mental disorders.

psychology: The broad study of the mind and behavior.

residency: A period of training in a hospital, done after a doctor graduates from medical school.

separation anxiety: Extreme nervousness that a person feels when she is separated from someone to whom she is very attached.

toxin: A poisonous substance.

127

BACKSTORIES

Uncover the epic histories of your favorite characters!

Read them all!